All About
YOU

All About
YOU

•••

2500 QUESTIONS
TO HELP YOU DISCOVER
WHO YOU REALLY ARE
(and have fun doing it)

HERRON

Introduction

How often is it all about you? With this book it is – 100%. With 2500 questions to contemplate, it will help you on the path to greater self-knowledge and awareness.

Some questions are deep, some are cheeky, some are fun and others are deadly serious. Hide out in your bedroom to really think about your answers, or chuck the book in your bag for fun moments chatting with friends. Everyone will learn something new about someone!

We had fun writing these questions for you, and we hope you have fun answering them. Be honest – and see where it takes you.

1. Do you fear for the planet?

2. When did you last feel sad? What about?

3. Will robots serve you at the checkout in your lifetime?

4. When is power bad?

5. What are some things you do with your pets?

6. What do you think about animals being in captivity?

7. What beverage could you not live without?

8. What do you do when you feel bored?

9. What have you learned that you think will be the most useful for your life?

10. What is under your bed?

11. What does self-care mean to you?

12. What makes you laugh?

13. How tall would you like to be, if you could choose?

14. If you could visit any planet, where would you go and why?

15. What makes you feel good about yourself?

16. Do you like your voice?

17. Do you tell your parents you love them?

18. How many bones are there in the human body?

19. Are you scared of spiders?

20. Do you know the Aboriginal name of the Country you live on?

21. What was the last disagreement you had with your siblings about?

22. Are you usually the person who cares the most or the least in your group?

23. Do you enjoy dating?

24. When will the world end?

25. If you believe in God does that mean God exists?

26. Are you a leader or a follower?

27. What personality traits do you dislike in others?

28. Who pays your phone bill?

29. If you were the Prime Minister and needed three people to assist you, who would you pick and why?

30. If you could design the ultimate treehouse, what would it look like?

31. Do you think coffee and caffeine are drugs?

32. How often does your extended family get together?

33. Where would your dream school trip be to and what would you do there?

34. Would you rather ace school or be average in school and master skills for the outside world?

35. Do you like the place where you grew up?

36. Do any of your friends suffer from mental health problems?

37. How would you describe yourself in five words or fewer?

38. What artistic medium do you prefer?

39. If a friend is stressed, how do you help them feel better?

40. Who is the smartest person you know?

41. What do you think about organised religion?

42. Who is your least favourite teacher this year?

43. Do you think the world would be a better place without the internet?

44. What makes a good friend?

45. How do you approach revision?

46. If you were a bird what kind you would be?

47. Do women have equal rights?

48. When do you feel a teen becomes an adult?

49. Do you feel like a responsible young adult?

50. What's your biggest regret in life so far?

51. When or how did you learn about sex?

52. What would you do if you ran into your parents on a first date?

53. Do you make to-do lists?

54. Who knows you best in the world?

55. What's been on your mind most lately?

56. Do you have any role models? Who and why?

57. Would you rather be the oldest child or the youngest child?

58. Do guns protect people?

59. How many times its body weight can an ant lift?

60. Would you rather wash your body with shampoo or your hair with soap?

61. What was the last sweet text you screenshotted and saved?

62. Is there something you wish your parents had pushed you harder to stick at?

63. If you had an envelope with your death date inside, would you open it?

64. Would you rather have to listen to only Lil Nas X or only Ariana Grande for the rest of your life?

65. Would you rather eat your favourite meal every day or never eat it again?

66. What do you consider the most beautiful thing about your personality?

67. What are some of your best childhood memories with cousins?

68. How would you explain 'love' to someone without using the word?

69. When at the movies, what is your favourite snack food?

70. Is it possible to think about nothing?

71. Which Mexican food has a name meaning 'little donkey'?

72. What's the best thing you ever bought online?

73. What's your favourite party outfit?

74. Did you meet anyone new today? What were they like?

75. Do you prefer friends similar to you or quite different?

76. Is it ever OK to break the law?

77. If you were given the option to give $10 million to charity or take $5 million for yourself, which would you choose?

78. Can people change?

79. What do you think you will achieve in your career?

80. What's the best teen party you've been to and why?

81. What was your first pet as a kid, and what happened to them?

82. Are you happy with your weight?

83. Do you prefer to travel alone or with friends?

84. Why is Pokémon so successful?

85. Would you rather have bad hair days for a week or wear extremely uncomfortable underwear for a day?

86. Do straight white men still hold the power in society?

87. Do soulmates exist?

88. Do you check your Insta stories to see if someone specific watched them?

89. Are you neurodiverse or neurotypical?

90. What do your friends say about you?

91. Do you believe in luck?

92. If you had the chance to be reborn as someone else, who would it be?

93. Why are mental health problems on the rise in society?

94. What type of film do you like most?

95. What music makes you happy?

96. In which cities can you imagine yourself living?

97. Would you rather be a famous celebrity or a life-saving fire fighter?

98. What's your favourite thing to do alone?

99. What's the most embarrassing thing you've done to get the attention of someone you liked?

100. How is your posture?

101. What is your happiest memory?

102. Would you rather be stuck with pirates on a ship or aliens on a spaceship?

103. Do you ever feel jealous about the family of any of your friends?

104. How many boyfriends or girlfriends have you had?

105. Do you think that everyone should be free to dress however they want?

106. Would you rather be a famous musician or a famous actor?

107. Would you rather live the rest of your life without your TV or your phone?

108. How have you coped with rejection?

109. What exotic cuisine do you like the most?

110. What one song would you choose to describe your life right now?

111. What is your biggest worry in life?

112. Would you rather never again touch your pet or the TV remote?

113. Will cars fly in your lifetime?

114. What celebrity have you imagined kissing?

115. Are you happy with your appearance?

116. Would you rather forget the name of a person you're on a date with or accidentally call them your ex's name?

117. Do you have faith?

118. Would you read a friend's (or siblings) journal?

119. What's the best gift you've ever given to your dad?

120. What scares you about the future?

121. Which of your friends knows the most about sport?

122. Would you rather go on a luxury vacation with family or a budget one with friends?

123. What is your favourite flavour of chips?

124. What is something you have always wanted to do?

125. Which is your ultimate takeaway meal and why?

126. What's your favourite meal of the day: breakfast, lunch or dinner?

127. What do you dream of doing when you're older?

128. What's the funniest YouTube channel?

129. Is it easier to love or be loved?

130. Have you ever seen a turtle swimming?

131. Which is the worse betrayal by a friend: lying to you or stealing from you?

132. What invention could you not live without?

133. Would you rather handwrite all your homework or use the computer to do it, but get a grade lower than you deserve?

134. What is the second-largest country in the world?

135. What is your strangest phobia?

136. When did you laugh the hardest?

137. At your school, are there a lot of people in romantic relationships?

138. What's your favourite thing in your bedroom?

139. If you could revive fashion trends from one decade, which would it be?

140. Have you ever been set up by a friend?

141. What's your favourite drink?

142. Are courage and bravery the same thing?

143. If your parents went away for a week and you had the house to yourself what would you do?

144. Are you looking forward to being an adult? Why?

145. Why do you think people like you?

146. How long does it take you to get ready in the morning?

147. Who was the last person you kissed?

148. Can money buy happiness?

149. What possessions do you value?

150. If you died today, is there anything you would regret?

151. If you could send one thought to a newborn baby, what would it be?

152. Can you remember your first day at primary school?

153. Do you process your emotions internally or by talking them through?

154. What is intuition?

155. Do you like how old you are now or do you wish you were older or younger?

156. Have you ever fallen asleep in class?

157. Do you like your house?

158. Would you rather date someone older or younger than you?

159. What's your favourite family memory?

160. What are the best and worst things about having a smartphone?

161. Do you like reading books?

162. Who do you turn to when you need advice?

163. Will you vote Labor, Liberal, Greens or something else?

164. What's the first thing you do when you go to the beach?

165. If you could design a national flag what would it be like?

166. Can you be too curious?

167. Do you have any frenemies?

168. Would you rather see 5 years into the future or 20 years into the future?

169. Which of your friends knows the most about literature?

170. How many pets do you want to have when you live on your own?

171. Can life be meaningful without friendship?

172. How long do you think you could be silent for?

173. How would your parents describe you as a baby?

174. Can you remember your favourite food as a kid?

175. Would you rather find out the tooth fairy is real or Santa Claus is real?

176. If you had a year to spend one million dollars, how would you spend it?

177. What do you think is most incredible about the universe?

178. What type of animal do you feel most connection with?

179. Have you ever felt betrayed by someone?

180. What makes you feel loved?

181. Who do you spend the most time with?

182. Do you save money every month or only when you have extra?

183. Who is your hero and why?

184. When did you have your first kiss, and with who?

185. If you could be invisible for a single day, what would you do?

186. Should people have to pay for education?

187. Have you ever been in love?

188. Do you have a secret ambition?

189. Are you good at taking feedback?

190. Do you shop online?

191. What is happiness to you?

192. Do you BookTok?

193. How would your parents describe you in your early teens?

194. If you could change one thing about yourself, what would it be?

195. What is your favourite snack to eat?

196. Would you swim with dolphins?

197. What is the best age to have kids?

198. Would you like to work for yourself?

199. If you and your friends won a $250 prize, how would you spend it?

200. Are you a good dancer?

201. What are three things that you are grateful for today or this week?

202. Would you rather help your crush or best friend pass an exam?

203. Were you bored today? Why do you think that is?

204. When is the last time you have been disappointed?

205. When do you think someone is ready to try alcohol?

206. If you could ask your favourite celebrity one thing, what would you ask?

207. If two people like each other romantically, do you think they should ask before trying to kiss?

208. What song could you listen to on repeat for the rest of your life?

209. What fiction author would you like to have a cup of tea and chat with?

210. If you could be the main character of any movie, what movie would it be?

211. Should everyone earn the same amount of money?

212. At what age would you like to live on your own?

213. Would you rather only be able to charge your phone once a week or not have a camera on your phone?

214. Would you rather burn to death or freeze to death?

215. What vegetable is your least favourite and why?

216. Who is your favourite artist?

217. If you could be any object, which would you be and why?

218. What was your most awkward moment on a date?

219. What do you think about drinking at parties?

220. Do you have good personal hygiene?

221. What do you think makes a good friend?

222. Who is your tribe?

223. How good is your memory?

224. How would you spend your free time if you could never watch TV or go online ever again?

225. Did anything funny happen at school today?

226. Should euthanasia be legal?

227. What is something you wish you were better at?

228. What big experiences do you think have most impacted your life so far?

229. Which choices have taught you the biggest lessons?

230. Do you think it's important to be able to speak other languages?

231. Would you ever swim with sharks?

232. Do the ends ever justify the means?

233. Would you go white-water rafting?

234. What's the biggest lesson you have learned about relationships?

235. Are you kind to yourself?

236. If you could choose (at no cost) between having a live-in chef, personal stylist, chauffeur, assistant or massage therapist, which would you go for?

237. Can you confidently cook for yourself?

238. Do you like spicy food?

239. Can you do a headstand?

240. Can you explain what climate change is?

241. Who is the nicest person you know?

242. Who is your favourite musician or band?

243. Would you be a good professional negotiator?

244. Would you rather eat the same dinner for the rest of your life or give up social media?

245. What's more important: doing the right thing or doing things right?

246. When did you have good luck?

247. Do you prefer boy bands or punk rock?

248. Does anyone in your family live overseas?

249. What do you like to cook?

250. What is the best conversation you have had recently?

251. What is something only you can do?

252. Would you rather be an Instagram influencer or YouTube famous?

253. Who do you fear the most?

254. What would help you feel more supported in life?

255. When do you do your homework?

256. How do you respond when a friend asks you to do something you don't want to do?

257. Is money important to you?

258. What do you need right now that you don't have?

259. Would you steal to feed a starving child?

260. Would you go to the moon if you could?

261. What confuses you?

262. What beauty or fashion moment do you regret most?

263. Which teacher at your school is the scariest?

264. If you could only eat at one restaurant for the rest of your life, which would you choose?

265. Where do you like to sit in class?

266. What would you call your future kids?

267. What's good about being an adult?

268. What qualities would you look for in a potential partner?

269. If you were invisible, where would you go?

270. If you could swap places with a prince or princess, would you?

271. What's the difference between art and science?

272. Do you think adults praise kids too much or not enough?

273. What would be the best thing about living by yourself?

274. What do you like in a sandwich?

275. Do you think people are born positive or negative in their outlook?

276. Are you good with money?

277. Would you rather go to school four days a week for 10 hours or five days a week for 8 hours?

278. How long do you spend on your phone each day?

279. What historical figure do you most identify with?

280. What is the last thing that you and your best friend fought about?

281. What movie absolutely scarred you?

282. Do you feel comfortable at family gatherings?

283. If you could choose, would you be an eagle or a kookaburra?

284. Who are your favourite creators on TikTok?

285. What have you recently lost interest in?

286. Have you ever failed a test? Which subject was it, and how did you feel?

287. How do you think you have changed since you started high school?

288. Do you live close to your extended family?

289. What's your favourite constellation?

290. Are you trustworthy?

291. What bands are you listening to these days?

292. How many Dreamtime stories do you know?

293. Would you rather drink coffee or tea for the rest of your life?

294. What do you think about politics?

295. What are you saving up to buy at the moment?

296. What's something you can do today that would make you feel good?

297. What clubs or activities do you participate in?

298. What are three very fun sports for you?

299. What is one problem with modern life?

300. What terrifies you, but you pretend to be brave about it?

301. What did you do today that made you feel good?

302. If you were to pick up a wallet filled with cash, would you keep it or try to find the owner?

303. What's the most helpful thing you do around the home?

304. Do you have the same hobbies as your friends?

305. What type of restaurant would you own?

306. Do you have a self-care routine?

307. What would your weapon of choice be in a zombie apocalypse?

308. Do you spend money impulse shopping or save for something specific?

309. Do you trust your head or your heart more?

310. Would you rather control King Kong or Godzilla?

311. Which day from your childhood do you wish you could relive?

312. Do you want to go away for uni?

313. What would you say is one of your weaknesses?

314. What do you think about your parents' approach to discipline?

315. What's the most dangerous hobby you have?

316. How have you had your hopes dashed before?

317. What's a career that doesn't exist (yet) that you think should? Would you want the job?

318. How would you describe your school?

319. Why don't they have seat belts on buses?

320. What do you think happens after death?

321. Do you think that you need a purpose in life?

322. What three things do you have in common with your sibling?

323. Would you rather win a laptop of choice or go on a free city break?

324. Would you rather throw an epic pool party and have to clean up an epic mess by yourself or not have the party at all?

325. Is it more important to be smart or clever?

326. Are you an ethical person? How do you know?

327. What personality traits make a good person?

328. How would you want to be remembered?

329. Are there time travellers living among us?

330. What's the scariest dream you've ever had?

331. If you could choose one of your toys to come to life, which would it be?

332. Would you rather be five years older or younger?

333. If your roommate on school camp was snoring what would you do?

334. Are you satisfied with the number and quality of your friendships?

335. Have you ever snuck out at night without your parents knowing?

336. Do you ever worry about being addicted to drugs or alcohol?

337. What kind of place do you think the world will be 25 years from now?

338. If you had to get rid of every possession except what would fit in a backpack, what would be in that backpack?

339. What excites you about your future?

340. Are you reading anything enjoyable right now?

341. What is the most embarrassing thing that has happened to you?

342. What are you most likely to argue about?

343. Would you rather be 30 or 18 forever?

344. Do you have any regrets?

345. Do you like your bedroom?

346. What's your favourite album right now?

347. How would you describe your parents' relationship?

348. What is the worst food in the world?

349. Do you feel safe?

350. If God is good, why does evil exist?

351. Where do you go shopping for your clothes?

352. How did you find out Santa wasn't real?

353. If you could be in any movie, which one would it be?

354. What leadership positions have you had so far, if any?

355. What word would you add to the dictionary and what does it mean?

356. What toppings do you love on ice cream?

357. What's the worst thing you've ever spent money on?

358. What is your dream trip?

359. What characteristics make a good leader?

360. Would you rather no lollies on Halloween or no presents on Christmas?

361. What is the last song you sang out loud?

362. What book would you want to actually get lost in?

363. Are your parents usually right?

364. What do you think is the biggest issue that teenagers face right now?

365. When were you bored today?

366. What is something you really want to do that's against your family rules?

367. How do you relax?

368. What superstition do you think is most ridiculous?

369. How far away is the moon?

370. What are three things you want to do this summer?

371. Who is your oldest friend?

372. Do you think we should talk more about race?

373. What is your reaction when you win or succeed?

374. What do you think is the most important quality in a teacher and why?

375. Does life have a meaning?

376. Do you believe in witchcraft?

377. What do you think is most important when it comes to dating?

378. Do you have a phone?

379. Do you think everyone has the right to do what they want with their body?

380. Would you rather adopt a cat or dog or buy a puppy or kitten?

381. What are the first three things you do when you get to school?

382. What is your favourite sport to watch?

383. Do you value honesty or humour more?

384. Do you meditate?

385. Would you ever drink pickle juice?

386. What is often your first thought in the morning?

387. What do you think about majority rule?

388. What is a habit you are most embarrassed by?

389. Would you rather have an exciting date or a romantic date?

390. Do you have trouble forgiving yourself for something?

391. Have you kissed a member of the same sex?

392. What were some of the best birthday presents you ever received?

393. What's your favourite fresh herb?

394. Which TV or movie character would you be friends with IRL?

395. What is the most annoying word in the English language?

396. What is something that you don't like doing but are good at?

397. Do you have fun at school?

398. How would you dress if you had no budget?

399. If you could know the future, would you choose to find out?

400. Do you believe in second chances?

401. What technological invention do you think the world needs?

402. How do you feel about public speaking?

403. On a scale of 1 (not a lot) to 10 (a lot), how much do you (honestly) care about your appearance?

404. What are some funny family stories you remember?

405. What's your favourite thing about your best friend?

406. What family rituals does your family have?

407. What's the best decision you ever made?

408. Are you scared of the ocean?

409. Which emojis do you use the most?

410. Would you rather be a surgeon or a pilot?

411. What do you do with the majority of your money?

412. If you could plan a special day for your bestie and money was no object, what would you do?

413. How do you measure success?

414. Would you rather be an amazing writer or a maths whizz?

415. What genre of music is your favourite at the moment?

416. Is maths a creative subject?

417. What does your dream future look like?

418. If you had to move to another country tomorrow, where would you go?

419. What weird or useless talent do you have?

420. Do you usually arrive places early, on time or late?

421. If you could take only one person on an all-expenses-paid overseas trip, who would it be?

422. Would you rather have bad long-term memory or bad short-term memory?

423. Have you ever ridden a horse?

424. Would you like to flat-share or live alone?

425. Has anyone ever told you something about yourself that surprised you?

426. Would you like to go on a safari?

427. If you joined the circus, what would your circus act be?

428. Do you believe in fate?

429. Why is 6 afraid of 7?

430. Would you rather tour with a famous band or a famous comedian?

431. What old person tendencies do you have?

432. What was the last concert you went to?

433. If you could paint your room any colour, which would you choose?

434. Would you rather date someone gorgeous but lacking a sense of humour or someone average-looking but hilarious?

435. Which class are you learning the least in?

436. What do you wish you knew how to do that you can't (yet)?

437. Would you rather sing or be in a spelling bee in front of the school?

438. Are you happy in your gender?

439. Are you a socialist?

440. What are numbers?

441. What is something that you feel passionately about in life?

442. What animal makes you giggle?

443. Have you ever spied on someone?

444. Would you rather play your favourite sports outdoors or stay indoors and play video games?

445. Do you plan social events with friends or just go along when invited?

446. What are your thoughts on marriage?

447. Where do our personalities come from?

448. What more do you think we should be doing to care for the planet?

449. Are you kind?

450. How are you in a crisis?

451. Do you think homework is helpful? If so, why? If not, what would you replace it with?

452. Do you like buying gifts for people?

453. Do you think your parents treat you (and your siblings) fairly?

454. Do you think a full moon affects your mood?

455. Do you remember facts or experiences better?

456. Did you ever spread a nasty rumour about someone else?

457. Is there anything you are looking forward to right now?

458. Where do you want to visit in the future?

459. How many times should you use a disposable razor?

460. Who are you closest to in your family?

461. Do you have any study goals for the year?

462. What is the best picture you have ever drawn?

463. Who would you say is your best friend right now?

464. Will humans eventually learn how to live forever?

465. Did you go to daycare or preschool?

466. Do you like music festivals?

467. Do you find it easy to be vulnerable?

468. What is the worst thing that's happened to you, and what did you learn from it?

469. What's your zodiac sign?

470. Did your grandmother/s work outside the home?

471. Do you have a growth mindset?

472. What is the most adventurous thing you have ever done in your life?

473. What did you do for your last birthday?

474. Do you have a bucket list? What are the top two or three things on it?

475. If you could ban one thing from school, what would it be?

476. If you could only communicate with one other person for the rest of your life, who would it be?

477. If you were in a play, what would your character be like?

478. Who do you eat lunch with at school?

479. What's your most creative accomplishment?

480. How do you handle change?

481. Would you rather spend a day with your favourite movie star or athlete?

482. What is humanity's biggest mistake so far?

483. What is your dream career?

484. Are places with fun things to do better than places where you can chat with friends and just chill?

485. What would you like to learn how to do?

486. Is everyone's life worth the same?

487. What's the best money you've ever spent?

488. What do you like the most about your schedule this year?

489. How many hours a week do you spend online?

490. How does a beautiful sunset make you feel?

491. How would you describe your relationship with your dad?

492. Is it better to have loved and lost than never to have loved at all?

493. Do you clash with anyone at school or in your friendship group?

494. Where's the first place you'd drive after getting your license?

495. Who do you think looks up to you?

496. Do you feel ready to date?

497. Would you rather marry someone who is entirely the opposite of you or exactly like you?

498. Are there any public holidays that you wish never existed?

499. Is there a celebrity that you are related to, no matter how distantly?

500. Do you want to have kids?

501. Are you a patient person?

502. What can you do today that you could not a year ago?

503. Are you worried about your future?

504. Do you ever get bored on the weekend?

505. Are men and women different?

506. Do schools do enough to support kids with mental health problems?

507. Does your name influence your personality?

508. Would you rather get paid $100 an hour and go to a physical office or $75 and work from home?

509. Do you prefer sunset or sunrise?

510. Who is your messiest friend?

511. Would you rather be invisible or be able to fly?

512. What do you think holds you back from doing the things you dream about?

513. What are the big things being talked about at school at the moment?

514. Is it more awkward to address adults as Mr/Ms or use their first names?

515. What is the best thing you've ever done?

516. Are you a thinker or a doer?

517. Have you ever been foraging for food?

518. What instrument do you think is the most annoying?

519. Would you ever get a tattoo?

520. If you were going to get one, what tattoo would you get? Why?

521. Would you rather have $10 million in ten years or $1 million today?

522. Would you prefer a faux fur or velvet couch?

523. Would you rather be unpopular and have real friends or be popular and have fake friends?

524. How do you end an annoying conversation?

525. Do you like dressing up?

526. Did you ever skip school and lie about it to your parents?

527. Would you break up with someone by sending them a text?

528. Who are your heroes and what qualities do you admire about them?

529. Is stealing always wrong?

530. Would you want to be famous?

531. What's the best thing about your neighbourhood?

532. Is it important for you to vote?

533. How many of your friends are the same religion as you?

534. Do you suffer from anxiety?

535. What do you eat too much of?

536. What would you do after graduation if money weren't a factor and nothing bad could happen?

537. What's the best piece of advice you've ever received?

538. Have you been kissed yet?

539. What is the point of Easter?

540. Have you ever learned a new skill and then realised you hated it?

541. What's the best musical you've ever seen?

542. Are you adventurous?

543. What attracts two people to each other?

544. If you worked really hard and won an award, what would it be for?

545. If you could be any emoji, which one would you be?

546. Do you know how your parents met?

547. What are you most attracted to in another person?

548. What is your comfort movie? TV show?

549. If your friends could have a teenage retreat, what would it be like?

550. What was your childhood nickname?

551. Do you know your purpose?

552. What is the point of education?

553. Would you rather give up peanut butter or Nutella?

554. When did you stop believing in fairies?

555. Are you a thrill-seeker?

556. Is time travel possible?

557. What do you want to do for your next birthday?

558. What is something that you learned how to do last summer?

559. What is the human body made of?

560. How would you describe your dad?

561. If you could choose your teachers for each subject, who would you want?

562. Do you have any enemies?

563. What are the best fireworks you've ever seen?

564. If your date had food in their teeth, would you tell them?

565. What do you pretend doesn't matter to you, but it really does?

566. What's the most unusual thing in your school bag right now?

567. Have you ever gambled?

568. What is the cruellest thing you have ever done?

569. What one thing do you really want but can't afford?

570. What do you admire most about your dad?

571. If you were given the chance to become immortal, would you take it?

572. Where do you most want to travel to?

573. What is your Chinese zodiac sign?

574. Would you rather have an American accent or a British accent?

575. What is your favourite soft drink?

576. What animal would scare you the most if you saw it in the wild?

577. Do you have any friends who live in other countries?

578. Who do you wish you were more like?

579. Do you overreact – never, sometimes, often?

580. Have you ever been a school representative?

581. Would you rather have no arms or no legs?

582. How do you prefer to be comforted when you're upset?

583. What is your favourite photo of yourself as a kid?

584. Are there any TV shows you like to watch with your family?

585. Can you imagine the house you will live in when you are middle-aged?

586. What do you get in trouble for most often?

587. What scares you the most about getting older?

588. What's a hobby that you don't currently have that you'd love to learn?

589. What would you do with a billion dollars?

590. Would you ever date someone with different religious beliefs than you?

591. Do you have a favourite uncle or aunt?

592. Do you think your family has enough money?

593. What's good about social media?

594. Which historical figure has had the biggest impact on the world?

595. Are you a partying kind of person?

596. Have you made a plan for your life?

597. Would you rather drink hot chocolate or eat chocolate pudding for a week?

598. What is your school mascot?

599. What is your favourite thing to do with your friends?

600. Is there a cause you would give up your life for?

601. What makes you sad?

602. What was a recent change you made that improved your life?

603. Have you ever struggled to forgive but felt better when you did?

604. If you had to curate the soundtrack to your life, what songs would be on there?

605. Are you ambitious?

606. What program or club do you wish your school had more money for?

607. Is being an influencer a real job?

608. What do you collect, and why?

609. Are you close with your neighbours?

610. Where do you love to hang out during the morning?

611. If you had just 24 hours to live, how would you spend your day?

612. What is your idea of heaven?

613. What will you wear on your wedding day?

614. Would you rather realise halfway through a date that there's something in your teeth or something in your nose?

615. What is the most expensive spice in the world?

616. What are your nervous habits when you are worried?

617. Are you into sports?

618. What makes you so awesome?

619. What do you dislike about your daily routine?

620. What is infinity?

621. Would you rather ask someone out or have someone ask you out?

622. Which subject do you think would be the most fun to teach?

623. When you leave high school what will you miss?

624. What is one invention you think should be created this year?

625. Would you rather visit every amusement park in the world or every national park in the world?

626. What is your saddest memory?

627. What are your goals for this year?

628. What was the first thing that made you laugh today?

629. What pet would you most like to have?

630. Have you ever worked for free?

631. Do you know anyone who is autistic?

632. What advice would you give adults about how to help kids navigate the online world?

633. Which of the five senses would you give up, if you could choose?

634. If you were on a game show, which charity would you compete for?

635. What job did your grandfather/s have?

636. Can a person live a happy life without hope?

637. Do you prefer gaming or social media?

638. Why is it hard to talk to your parents?

639. What is something you wish more people knew about you?

640. What would society be better without?

641. How do you know what is real?

642. What is the most embarrassing thing your parents caught you doing?

643. What movie would you like to see turned into a musical?

644. What body part do you think is most useless?

645. What food would you eat for the rest of your life if you could only choose one?

646. Do animals experience love?

647. Are you good at maths?

648. What's taking up most of your headspace right now?

649. Which possession do you cherish the most? Why?

650. Can you whistle in tune?

651. What favourite project are you working on right now?

652. Does your family have any hidden secrets?

653. What quotes from movies, songs or books do you really like?

654. What are you hoping for from life?

655. What's the worst thing about being a teenager?

656. Who always makes you feel better when you're feeling down?

657. Are you a lover or a fighter?

658. What is a memorable act of kindness you have witnessed? How did it affect you?

659. Would you ditch lunch plans with your bestie to go on a date?

660. If you could make up a spell, what would it do?

661. Do you like running?

662. If you go to a new place where there are animals, do you go up to the animals to say hi or keep clear?

663. What animal represents you the best?

664. Do you agree with the current legal age for smoking?

665. Would you rather have a mansion or a private jet?

666. If you were going to bury a time capsule, what would you put in it?

667. What job would you be terrible at?

668. What is your favourite place on earth?

669. Why did your parents give you your name?

670. What's the best project or activity you've done at school?

671. What is the weirdest thing you have ever eaten?

672. How old should a person be when they leave home?

673. What is your communication style?

674. Would you rather have no sense of taste or not see what you eat?

675. Did you have a bike, scooter, roller skates or all of the above as a kid?

676. What do you do as soon as you wake up?

677. When was the last time you told someone you loved them?

678. Do you take care of yourself physically?

679. Would you rather be trapped in a horror movie with your friends or a romantic comedy with your enemies?

680. Is society inherently good?

681. What would you put in a time capsule?

682. Do you have a role model?

683. Have you ever been made fun of at school?

684. If you could get an important message across to a large group of people what would it be?

685. What is the most important part of school?

686. If you could live one day all over again, which would you choose?

687. When are you most likely to cry?

688. What does your ultimate birthday party look like?

689. What would you do if a friend was in trouble with drugs?

690. Is the grass always greener on the other side?

691. When did you not speak up but wish you had?

692. What has been the scariest experience of your life so far?

693. Would you rather meet someone new every day or watch a new movie every day?

694. Who is the first person you text when you get bad news?

695. What was the last thing that made you cry?

696. Can you define 'the soul'?

697. What is your theory of why the chicken crossed the road?

698. Would you use a dating website?

699. What makes your friends so awesome?

700. What are you most excited to do this school year?

701. What do you like to watch on YouTube?

702. Which TV show do you wish they would bring back?

703. What would make you jump out of bed at 6 am on a Saturday?

704. What do you use to take notes in class?

705. Would you rather always be cold or always be hot?

706. If you have been taught about online safety and media literacy at school, did you learn anything useful?

707. What makes you angry and why?

708. At what age should you be allowed to stay out all night?

709. Where would you like to get married?

710. Would you rather lose your phone or your keys?

711. What are you doing next weekend?

712. What would you do to change your room?

713. What's one book that changed your life?

714. If you had to cut off all communication with a close family member for five years, who would it be?

715. Can an opinion ever be wrong?

716. What's your favourite tree?

717. If you could accomplish one feat to help the world, what would it be?

718. Is it possible to levitate?

719. What's your favourite book of all time?

720. If you could have three wishes, what would they be?

721. Would you rather have super strength or super hearing?

722. Do you feel judged by your parents sometimes?

723. Would you rather have no tests or no homework?

724. Would you rather hit the pause button on your life or the rewind button?

725. What's the most interesting assignment you've worked on this year?

726. Do you expect to go to university?

727. What is a magical power that you wish you had?

728. Can you tell when someone is lying?

729. Who is your favourite actor?

730. Would you rather be a mouse or an elephant?

731. Do you feel you have more freedom to be yourself with your friends?

732. Would you rather tell on your best friend or your sibling?

733. Are there any kinds of food you want to pack more for lunch this year?

734. If you could delete all social media apps and go off the grid, would you?

735. Would you rather create a famous invention or a piece of art?

736. What will you miss most when you leave home?

737. Which of your friends is kindest?

738. Would you rather never eat tomato sauce again or put it on everything?

739. Would you rather watch all the *Harry Potter* or *Star Wars* movies?

740. Are there parts of your body that you dislike?

741. How is love different from desire?

742. How's your love life?

743. Can robots experience consciousness?

744. What is a deal-breaker for you when it comes to new people?

745. What personality traits are most important to you in a boyfriend or girlfriend?

746. Which is better: home or someplace new?

747. What's illegal that should not be?

748. If you were a pair of shoes, what kind would you be?

749. What are some things that are best left unsaid?

750. Are you conventional or unconventional?

751. Do you have a favourite movie?

752. What's the weirdest thing a teacher has done in class?

753. Would you rather your family were like the Addams Family or the Brady Bunch?

754. How important is it to be financially secure?

755. If you had to go out on a date with a friend, who would it be?

756. What do you take really seriously?

757. What or who would you be willing to give up everything you own for?

758. Which public holidays do you really like and why?

759. What's your favourite game?

760. Would you be willing to die for your best friend?

761. Which of your friends knows the most about astrology?

762. What is the grossest food in the canteen? Does anyone like it?

763. What's your favourite flower?

764. How would you explain Earth and humans to an alien?

765. Would you get your body frozen after death?

766. If you had to be a mythical creature, what would you be?

767. Is there ever a time when giving up makes sense?

768. Would you rather win $3,000 in the lottery every month or work and earn $5,000 every month?

769. Do you know any pick-up lines?

770. Have you ever wanted to be (more) popular?

771. If you could buy anything in the world right now what would it be?

772. Do you think it's better to have one outstanding skill or lots of competent skills? Why?

773. What would your autobiography be called and why?

774. What's the worst TV ad you've seen recently?

775. Do you know what your values are?

776. What's a lesson you've had to learn the hard way?

777. Can you change the course of your life?

778. Can you tell the difference between different accents in English?

779. What were some of the best Christmas presents you ever received?

780. Would you rather own a magic wand or a lightsaber?

781. Would you rather be able to fly or breathe underwater?

782. If you were told you would live forever, what would you change about your life?

783. How old do you want to be when you get married?

784. What would turn you off someone on a date?

785. What are you most looking forward to about being an independent adult?

786. How do you think your friends feel about school?

787. What's your greatest strength and your greatest weakness?

788. Do you believe in horoscopes?

789. Would you rather be good at synchronised swimming or chess?

790. What role would you have in a rock band?

791. Do you read the news?

792. What tech do you wish you owned?

793. What part of your childhood are you most nostalgic for?

794. What have you done in the last year to be proud of?

795. What's the worst miscommunication you've had with a friend?

796. What do you think are the most beautiful animals?

797. Are you a persuasive person?

798. Where do you spend the majority of your waking hours?

799. If you could drop one class at school without consequence, which one would it be?

800. What bunch of flowers would you most like to receive?

801. Are you good at making decisions?

802. What's your most embarrassing moment from high school?

803. Does everybody see colours the same?

804. What's the most spontaneous thing you have ever done?

805. What's inside your dream home?

806. What is the weirdest or craziest thing you have ever done?

807. If you had the power, what would you do about teen mental health problems?

808. What's your favourite childhood memory with your mum?

809. Are you a relaxed person?

810. What was the worst day of your life and why?

811. What three things do you have in common with your dad?

812. Do you care about what other people think about you?

813. If you could learn the answer to one of history's great mysteries which would it be?

814. What is the most embarrassing thing that your mum does?

815. Are we too greedy as humans?

816. Do you try to eat well?

817. What is the strangest thing you've ever had for breakfast?

818. Do you believe in karma?

819. Would you rather scuba-dive or go on safari?

820. How confident are you about achieving your dreams?

821. What's your favourite thing about autumn?

822. What's something from your childhood you still like doing (even though you are maybe a bit too old)?

823. Do you sometimes say something that is different to what you mean?

824. Would you cheat to win a game for yourself?

825. Do you have a 'type'?

826. What is fake news?

827. What's your favourite smell?

828. What's the best thing in your life right now?

829. What was the last thing you downloaded?

830. If you could be born again as a creature which would you choose?

831. What is the silliest, most unreasonable fear you have?

832. Which is better: many friends, a few good friends or one dear friend?

833. Is organic food worth the cost?

834. Would you win an arm wrestle with Serena Williams?

835. Do you like olives?

836. Do you feel like you act differently when you're by yourself versus when you're with a group of people?

837. What makes you thrilled and excited?

838. What time do you get up on the weekend?

839. What's the first thing you notice when you meet a person?

840. Which songs get stuck in your head?

841. Is being well-mannered important in life?

842. If you could plan a special day for your family and money was no object, what would you do?

843. What do you find boring?

844. Do you agree with the current legal age for drinking?

845. Are you charming?

846. What's the latest you've been out at night?

847. What is your favourite fruit?

848. Do you ever feel lonely or left out?

849. Which is worse, failing or never trying?

850. Do you think people should be married to have sex?

851. Would you join the army?

852. Is your cup half full or half empty?

853. Would you rather be a famous songwriter or a famous drummer?

854. Do you think it's important to save for a rainy day?

855. What's something weird grownups regularly do?

856. Would you choose no enemies and one good friend, or a few enemies and many friends?

857. What is different about being in this school year versus the last one?

858. Who do you think is your celebrity look alike?

859. Would you eat raw garlic?

860. What was the last thought-provoking text you read?

861. Would you rather be able to play every instrument in the school orchestra or every position on the school football team?

862. Who gets the armrest on the middle seat?

863. What's the difference between love and lust?

864. What's your favourite show right now?

865. Is surrogacy ethical?

866. If you could have lunch with a Disney character who would you choose?

867. Are you more of an indoor person or an outdoor person?

868. What do you truly need in life?

869. At what age is a person considered elderly?

870. Would you prefer to hear the bad news first or the good news first?

871. What's more important to you: the past, present or future?

872. Could your grandmother drive a car?

873. What is at the bottom of the ocean?

874. If there were no physical, financial or other obstacles, what skill would you like to have?

875. Have you ever held a snake?

876. What do you think about the most during each day?

877. Who would be the worst person to be stuck in an elevator with?

878. What animals do you feel sorriest for at the zoo?

879. What will you miss when you are an adult?

880. Would you rather be rich or famous?

881. If you could describe your dad in three words, what would they be?

882. If you were the teacher at school tomorrow, what three things would you teach your class?

883. How long do you want to live?

884. What makes you lose interest in someone?

885. Would you ever kill someone?

886. What qualities do you admire in other people?

887. Do you take better care of your mind or your body?

888. Do you think sport should be obligatory at school?

889. Do you like busy places or quiet places?

890. Do you think exes can stay friends?

891. Are you dating someone right now?

892. What is something you would choose never to do again for the rest of your life?

893. If you could add a room to your house, what would it be for?

894. What do you wish your parents did differently?

895. If you could trade places for someone for the day, who would you choose?

896. If you could only describe yourself in three words, what would they be?

897. What's your love language?

898. Do you consider yourself a leader?

899. Would you rather date someone really quiet or someone really loud?

900. What's your favourite thing about spring?

901. Does life exist outside of Earth?

902. Should you be able to take your phone to school?

903. Would you rather wear the same socks for a month or the same underwear for a week?

904. What distracts you?

905. What things are you really into?

906. Who is stricter – your mum or dad?

907. What's the most annoying thing about the internet?

908. What thoughts keep you awake at night?

909. Which animal does Alice in Wonderland try to play croquet with?

910. What is your definition of success?

911. What's the proudest you've ever been of yourself?

912. Have you ever had a paying job?

913. How do you make the time pass on a long journey?

914. If you could only play one game for a whole year, which would you choose and why?

915. What do you need in order to fulfil your wishes for life?

916. How many kids do you want to have in the future?

917. What motivates you?

918. If you had one wish, what would you wish for?

919. What could society do without?

920. What activities do you like to do with your friends?

921. Do you like to spend time alone or prefer to be with friends?

922. Are you a good photographer?

923. What was the last thing you searched for on your phone?

924. Would you rather never lose a sports game or never lose an argument?

925. Do you prefer TV shows or movies?

926. What is your favourite way to chat to your friends: phone, text, online, in person?

927. Do you know how to turn the water off at the mains?

928. Would you rather eat at a restaurant or get take away?

929. What would be good about being Prime Minister?

930. Are you too nice?

931. What do you understand about yourself today that you didn't a year ago?

932. Can you be happy without ever falling in love?

933. Which charity would you donate $1 million to if you could?

934. Have you finished growing?

935. Which of your friends do you think will be famous?

936. Have you got a journal at home, and what do you write in it if you do?

937. Is there anyone you have a crush on right now?

938. If you had a time machine that could only work once, what point in the past or future would you visit?

939. What will cars be like 25 years from now?

940. What soothes you?

941. How would you describe your mum?

942. Do you think it's OK to have secrets in relationships?

943. Have you ever had a concussion?

944. What noise makes you cringe?

945. How do you look after yourself when you're a bit crook?

946. If you could give everyone in the world the same gift, what would it be?

947. Would you rather look bad in photos but take great ones or always look good but never take a decent one?

948. Which anime character would you like to be?

949. What are you grateful for right now?

950. What does your ideal weekend look like?

951. Does being in nature calm you?

952. Have you ever lent money (over $50)?

953. Do you think teens have it easier or tougher compared to their parents' generation?

954. If you had the chance to live on your own right now, would you take it?

955. Would you prefer ice cream cake or sponge cake for your next birthday?

956. Do you compare yourself to your friends?

957. Who's your favourite sibling?

958. What makes you feel energised?

959. Did you ever break your boyfriend's/girlfriend's heart?

960. If we learn the most from failure, why are we so afraid to fail?

961. What would you carve out of a block of ice?

962. Do you have trouble falling asleep?

963. Do you know anyone who you would say has an ideal relationship?

964. What was your best school camp so far?

965. If you had to pick one person to survive on a deserted island with, who would it be?

966. Where were your great-grandfathers born?

967. Did you like LEGO as a kid?

968. Would you rather own a restaurant or a retail store with your family?

969. What's the biggest threat to the environment?

970. Why do people get married?

971. Where would you most like to go partying?

972. Should people be allowed to sell their organs?

973. What would your ultimate vacation look like?

974. Would you rather live in a world where you sing instead of talk or dance instead of walk?

975. Who is your favourite actress?

976. Do you think you will live overseas one day?

977. How male or female do you feel inside as you get older?

978. What is something you've learned from friendship?

979. Have you passed up on any chances that you now regret?

980. How important is nature to you?

981. How do you think the universe came to be?

982. If a friend asked you to keep a secret that you don't feel comfortable keeping, what would you do?

983. Have you drunk alcohol?

984. Are you more like your mum or your dad?

985. What's a fun thing you do with your dad (or other older relative)?

986. Do you use nail scissors or nail clippers?

987. Who is your favourite cousin?

988. What do you wish was easier?

989. Do you feel comfortable in silence?

990. Which cartoon character do you wish was real?

991. Are your parents strict?

992. How big were you at birth?

993. How are you a good friend?

994. Would you rather date someone three feet taller or three feet shorter than you?

995. How many times have you been sent to the principal's office?

996. Which is worse: Brussels sprouts or broccoli?

997. Do you look forward to or dread sports at school?

998. What's the best thing about summer?

999. Who is your favourite character from a book?

1000. Are you shy?

1001. Are you crafty?

1002. If you dialled the wrong number at 2 am, would you rather it was your teacher or your ex you called?

1003. Are some people born evil?

1004. What is better than sliced bread?

1005. What's the worst thing about being a teenager?

1006. If you could communicate with an animal, which would you choose?

1007. Would you cheat to win a game for your team?

1008. Have you ever pretended to be sick so you can avoid a test?

1009. Have you ever let someone else take the flack for something you did?

1010. Would you trade your sibling for $1 million?

1011. Can you be happy if you've never been sad?

1012. Would you rather watch your dreams or control them?

1013. Is it more important that people like or respect you?

1014. What's your learning style (auditory, visual, etc)?

1015. What childhood event do you think most impacted you as a person?

1016. Would you rather have your grandmother or your grandfather follow you around school for the day?

1017. Are you a bright colours or neutrals kind of person?

1018. What's the worst decision you ever made?

1019. What three professions do you have a lot of respect for?

1020. Do you have any personal goals for yourself this year?

1021. What is the best thing about getting older?

1022. Where would you book tickets to if you could go anywhere in the world right now for free?

1023. Do you get an allowance? How much?

1024. Did you have an imaginary friend? What was his or her name?

1025. When you have free time what do you enjoy doing?

1026. How would you get your hair styled if you could do it any way?

1027. What do you consider red flags in relationships?

1028. If you had to describe yourself with a movie title, what would it be?

1029. Do you remove labels from clothes or do they not bother you?

1030. What are some of the first things that you remember?

1031. Would you rather take care of all the family pets or have no pets?

1032. Are you being bullied at the moment?

1033. Do you still enjoy 'family days'?

1034. Are you naturally smiley?

1035. Do you believe that the universe will provide?

1036. What is the app that you wish everyone had on their phone?

1037. If you could eat dinner with three people you don't know, who would they be and where would you go?

1038. Do you believe in hell?

1039. Would you rather sleep for 11 hours a day or four hours a day?

1040. What's the best roller coaster you've ever ridden?

1041. What is the difference between innocence and ignorance?

1042. Is there someone you're looking forward to seeing again?

1043. Would you rather have no hearing or no sight?

1044. If you could describe your mum in three words, what would they be?

1045. Do you think you could survive in prison?

1046. Do you wear make-up?

1047. What is the most important thing you learned in school NOT taught by a teacher?

1048. What did you do in the last 24 hours to make someone's life better?

1049. If you had an hour left to live, what would you do?

1050. Do you gravitate to younger or older people?

1051. What's a good alternative to God?

1052. Would you rather be stranded on a deserted island alone or with someone you dislike?

1053. Are you looking forward to leaving home?

1054. What was the stupidest thing you ever did?

1055. What three things do you have in common with your bestie?

1056. Have you ever had your Tarot cards read? What did they say?

1057. Who is the most handsome guy at school?

1058. Where do you hang out with your friends?

1059. What is your favourite joke?

1060. On a scale of 1–10 how important is family to you?

1061. What do you do for exercise?

1062. Do any types of conversations make you uncomfortable?

1063. If you could travel back in time three years, what advice would you give yourself?

1064. What's the weirdest thing you've ever bought?

1065. Would you rather be a princess or a mermaid?

1066. What five items would you grab if your house was on fire?

1067. Did you feel loved as a kid?

1068. What was the last thing you posted on Instagram?

1069. Would you rather ride a bike or a horse to work?

1070. Do you live by any life motto?

1071. If you had enough money that you never had to work, what would you do with your time?

1072. What's the best thing about your family?

1073. Would you rather be a pet dog or a wild wolf?

1074. Would you rather wear winter or summer clothes all year long?

1075. What's a memory that makes you happy?

1076. Are you similar to any of your grandparents? In what ways?

1077. Where would you like to go on a first date?

1078. Would you rather give up all books or all your gadgets?

1079. What's something you have in common with the person next to you?

1080. Do you sleep well?

1081. What do you think about on train journeys?

1082. Would you rather find true love or get all the material things you desire?

1083. What do you not understand but feel like you should?

1084. Do you still get excited about Christmas?

1085. What do you wish you'd done differently today?

1086. Would you rather have a video game come to life or get trapped inside one?

1087. What is something that upset you lately?

1088. What would you most like to accomplish in your favourite hobby?

1089. In your opinion, who is the coolest celebrity, and why?

1090. What is your favourite book right now?

1091. What activities does your family enjoy doing together?

1092. What sports interest you?

1093. If you found a remote that could rewind, fast-forward, stop and start time, what would you do with it?

1094. Do you sleep on your back, front or side?

1095. If you could have a celeb as your BFF, who would it be?

1096. What is one thing you learned today?

1097. What makes you nervous?

1098. Can teens go broke, and what happens then?

1099. Is being manipulative always a bad thing?

1100. Who do you most like to spend time with?

1101. What spots do you recommend most to relax at?

1102. Do you think there is likely to be any conflict in your group of friends this year?

1103. Would you disclose a friend's secret if they were in danger?

1104. What is most challenging in your life right now?

1105. Do you own any crystals?

1106. What is your favourite candle scent?

1107. How many people would you trust with your life?

1108. What's the best trip you've ever taken?

1109. If you could trade lives with a character in a book, who would it be?

1110. What do you call your grandparents?

1111. What's the bravest thing you've ever done?

1112. Would you rather be an only child or have ten siblings?

1113. Do you find routine relaxing or boring?

1114. If you could be famous for one thing, what would it be for and why?

1115. Would you rather die peacefully at 60 or painfully at 100?

1116. If you could pitch a show to Netflix that's guaranteed to be produced, what would it be about? What role would you play?

1117. Have you ever had a message from 'the other side'?

1118. If you got caught in the rain, would you splash in puddles or run for cover?

1119. Would you prefer to be buried or cremated?

1120. How old do you want to be when you have your first child?

1121. What single character trait would you like to be known for?

1122. Who's your favourite band or solo artist?

1123. Would you rather speak in front of 100,000 people for 1 minute or give a speech in front of your school for 30 minutes?

1124. What kind of a person would you want to be married to in the future?

1125. What news event has most shocked you?

1126. What is your favourite colour to wear?

1127. Do you have any phobias?

1128. Would you rather live in Melbourne or Sydney?

1129. Would you choose a different name for yourself? (What would it be?)

1130. Is there anything you're really stressed out about right now?

1131. Are you a resilient person or do you easily give up?

1132. What can you see from the window of your bedroom?

1133. What songs would you have on your wedding day?

1134. What's one of your fondest memories of growing up?

1135. Would you rather see any one day in the future or read minds for a day?

1136. If your friend did something really bad, would you cover for them or help them admit to it?

1137. Have you ever sent an embarrassing text message to the wrong person?

1138. Do you like talking about how you feel?

1139. In what ways do you think differently or the same as your parents?

1140. What upsets you?

1141. What's one thing that made you laugh recently?

1142. Are you a practical person?

1143. If you could drop one person in your life without consequence, who would it be?

1144. How do you think the world will end?

1145. Which is more important, being kind or getting even?

1146. What kind of music do you like?

1147. If death is inevitable, why bother doing anything?

1148. What is your favourite lolly?

1149. Do you feel you have the skills to cope with life?

1150. What advice about life would you give to others?

1151. Are you a romantic person?

1152. How would you spend a rainy day?

1153. Do you think you hold yourself back?

1154. What is a favourite memory you have of your friends?

1155. How does your family celebrate birthdays?

1156. Do you prefer to go out for hamburgers or pizza?

1157. Would you rather be turned down by someone you like or asked out by someone you don't?

1158. When is the last time you were super excited about something?

1159. What causes tides?

1160. Do you consider yourself to be a shy person or an outgoing person?

1161. If you were friends with a celebrity who would it be?

1162. Where do you feel the most comfortable?

1163. If someone asked you to go to a place you know is off-limits would you go anyway?

1164. Would you rather work at a bakery or an ice cream shop?

1165. Should gambling be banned?

1166. Do you go to church?

1167. What's your favourite beauty or grooming product?

1168. Do your parents restrict your internet access? Is it fair?

1169. When do you listen to music?

1170. Do you have siblings? Where are you in the birth order?

1171. Is family mealtime important?

1172. Are you gay, straight, queer, bi or rather not say?

1173. What was the most difficult thing you did today?

1174. What do you think about before going to sleep at night?

1175. Are very intelligent people happier than less intelligent people?

1176. What is your favourite outdoor activity?

1177. Is there anyone at school that you would like to get to know better? Who is it?

1178. Do you want to be wealthy when you're older?

1179. What three items would you take to a deserted island?

1180. Would you make a good housewife or househusband?

1181. Do you know what job you want to do?

1182. What are you proud of yourself for?

1183. Are you a spiritual person?

1184. Would you ever get a piercing?

1185. How do you discover new music?

1186. What or who is the biggest threat to society?

1187. If you could travel back in time to any moment in your life, which would you choose?

1188. What inspires you?

1189. Have aliens made it to Earth?

1190. Do you know any kids with two mums or two dads?

1191. Which of your parents are you most like?

1192. What product would you stockpile if you found out it was going to be phased out?

1193. Would you rather have pop-up ads or extremely slow internet?

1194. What kind of personalities make you feel uncomfortable to be around?

1195. Which astrological sign would you never want to date?

1196. What is most important to you in life?

1197. Do you have a favourite place in nature to visit?

1198. What does your body language say about you?

1199. What's the best prank that's been played on you?

1200. What is your favourite ice cream flavour?

1201. Do you play any musical instruments?

1202. What happens after we die?

1203. Do you prefer to take your time and write neatly or write fast so you can get the job done?

1204. What is something you wish your parents understood about you?

1205. Would you rather attend Hogwarts or be a Pokémon trainer?

1206. Do you study hard?

1207. What do you think is behind the teen mental health crisis?

1208. Is being psychic a real thing?

1209. What's the one thing adults really don't get about teenagers?

1210. What three apps do you need on your phone?

1211. Is there anything about your life that you'd like to change?

1212. What apps make you feel happy when you use them?

1213. Will your kids own their own home?

1214. Which family member are you most proud of?

1215. What's your favourite line from a movie?

1216. Where in Africa would you most like to travel?

1217. Can you usually remember the punchline to a joke?

1218. Do kids in school cheat on their tests or assignments? What do you think about that?

1219. Would you rather run barefoot over hot coals or broken glass?

1220. Who's your ultimate celeb crush?

1221. Does the music you listen to influence the clothes you wear?

1222. Do the smart kids have the best lives?

1223. How old are your parents?

1224. Is free internet a human right?

1225. Would you rather be a famous rapper or a famous pop star?

1226. Which theme park do you want to visit one day and why?

1227. How would you define your character?

1228. If you could write a book, what would it be about?

1229. What card games do you know how to play?

1230. What taste reminds you of your childhood?

1231. Are Sundays different from Saturdays for you?

1232. What is your big ambition?

1233. What is your perfect meal?

1234. What is something your family cares about, but you don't?

1235. Would you take your first boyfriend or girlfriend home?

1236. In what circumstances is it OK to question your elders?

1237. Have you ever made a friend on holiday?

1238. What is the worst grade you ever got in school?

1239. Are some memories more valuable than others?

1240. Have you ever played a prank on a teacher?

1241. Would you ever have cosmetic surgery?

1242. Does your family have any traditions?

1243. Who would narrate the audiobook of your life?

1244. What hurts your feelings?

1245. Have you ever tried to break a habit and succeeded?

1246. What's the hardest decision you've had to make?

1247. If you follow the news, where do you access it?

1248. Do you like to help out around the house?

1249. In what ways are you privileged?

1250. Can you do a cartwheel?

1251. What was your favourite game when you were a kid?

1252. Do you find it easy to make friends?

1253. Do you find making small talk with strangers easy or hard?

1254. What do you value most in friends?

1255. Should you forgive someone who cheats on you?

1256. What traits do you look for when you're trying to make a new friend?

1257. Are you naturally curious?

1258. What crime would you be arrested for?

1259. When you were younger, what did you want to be when you grew up?

1260. Who do you barrack for?

1261. Would you rather be the president of your student council or the most popular person in school?

1262. Are you a warm-weather or cold-weather person?

1263. What do you wish you were more motivated to do?

1264. Who do you most dislike and why?

1265. What was your biggest struggle at school?

1266. Have you been in any school plays?

1267. What's the best compliment you've ever received?

1268. In *Finding Nemo* what kind of fish is Dory?

1269. What is your favourite snack food?

1270. Where were your great-grandmothers born?

1271. What makes you feel brave?

1272. Do you like to keep your room neat and organised or do you prefer mess?

1273. Would you rather have your texts or your DMs made public?

1274. If you were to open a store, what would it sell?

1275. Would you rather have piercings or tattoos?

1276. If you could invite three people, living or dead, to your birthday party, who would you choose? What would you talk about or do?

1277. Are you a morning person?

1278. Do you like the way that you look?

1279. Do you prefer to surf or ski?

1280. When do you think it's OK to give up on a dream?

1281. What talents or skills do you have?

1282. If you could change anything about your childhood, what would it be?

1283. Why do people need friends?

1284. Does your attitude affect your ability?

1285. How do you handle stress?

1286. What three things can't you live without?

1287. What do you think about to make you get out of bed?

1288. Who was your first crush at school?

1289. What thing about your home do you find most annoying?

1290. What do you think makes your generation unique?

1291. Do you know anyone with an alcohol problem?

1292. Do you ever get sick of people asking you what job you want to do?

1293. Are you good at gardening?

1294. Which element (earth, water, fire, air) best describes you?

1295. Would you rather wear a clown's wig or their shoes every day?

1296. If you went on an African safari, which animal would you want to see?

1297. How often will you call your mum when you've left home?

1298. What's your favourite part of the day?

1299. Would you travel to a developing nation by yourself?

1300. What was a good conversation you had today?

1301. How are you in exams?

1302. Do you have a fixed phone line at home?

1303. What kind of tradie would you be?

1304. What places in the world are you curious about?

1305. What do you look forward to most each day?

1306. If you could wake up tomorrow fluent in two other languages, which would you choose and why?

1307. Do you think you'll still have the same friends in 25 years?

1308. What's been your worst family holiday?

1309. Would you rather be a popular person on social media or in school?

1310. Does an influential person influence everyone?

1311. What does it mean to say that 'if you point your finger at someone, three fingers are pointing back at you'?

1312. What job would you never do regardless of the money?

1313. Does power change people?

1314. Do you procrastinate?

1315. When have you felt let down?

1316. Who do you think loves you the most in the world?

1317. Would you prefer to live on a boat or on a remote island?

1318. Do you think social media helps make and/or maintain friendships?

1319. What is the one question you do not want to be asked in this book?

1320. Can you play a musical instrument?

1321. Do you give good advice?

1322. How do you want others to describe you?

1323. Out of all your family members, who are you the closest with?

1324. Do animals have souls?

1325. What's your biggest guilty pleasure?

1326. If you had to marry a celebrity who's a different gender than you are normally attracted to who would you pick?

1327. What are your grades like?

1328. What's the best birthday you've ever had?

1329. What does the perfect partner look like to you?

1330. If you were half person and half fish which would you want on the top half?

1331. Do you like tomatoes?

1332. Who do you look up to?

1333. What do you plan to do after you leave high school?

1334. Would you wear the same outfit for the rest of your life if someone paid you $1 million to do it?

1335. Would you rather win in the AFL grand final or the Australian Open?

1336. What have your past relationships taught you?

1337. What's the best gift you've ever given to your mum?

1338. What's your idea of a perfect date?

1339. Which is your favourite place to chill or hang out in town?

1340. Do you prefer people who are woke or ignorant?

1341. Is gender a social construct?

1342. What skill do you think you'll need when you leave home that you don't have yet?

1343. Are you a good friend to yourself?

1344. Who owes you an apology?

1345. What do you feel like other people judge you for?

1346. What is the last book you read?

1347. Do you create social media content?

1348. Who is your newest friend?

1349. Would you rather live in a world with no toilet paper or no soap?

1350. Have you ever written a love poem?

1351. Is cheating ever OK?

1352. How much would someone need to pay you to bungee jump?

1353. What hairstyles do you think kids of the future will be wearing?

1354. Have you ever enjoyed a poem in class but pretended it was lame?

1355. Would you rather be friends with the people from the school photography club or the football team?

1356. What makes you most afraid?

1357. Do you think art should be compulsory at school?

1358. Do you think you have enough free time?

1359. What's a fun thing you do with your mum (or female relative)?

1360. Which board game is your favourite to play with friends and family?

1361. What would you like to study at university?

1362. Are you a good writer?

1363. If not here, where would you be and what would you be doing at this moment?

1364. What was the most different thing about your childhood?

1365. If you could close your eyes and be somewhere else, where would you be?

1366. How would you describe the vibe of your family?

1367. What is the name of your favourite restaurant?

1368. Is bullying a problem at your school?

1369. What are the three most important qualities you look for in a friend?

1370. Would you rather eat meat for every meal or give up meat entirely?

1371. If you lived in a cave in the woods, what would be inside it?

1372. Would you rather throw your phone in the ocean or swim in a pool of mud?

1373. How gross are your school toilets?

1374. What are the most valuable life lessons you learned from your parents?

1375. Where would you like to travel to in the future?

1376. Are we alone in the universe?

1377. If you had to read only one celebrity memoir for the rest of your life, whose book would you choose?

1378. How would you describe your personal style?

1379. Are you the youngest in your family?

1380. Would you rather have a house with an aquarium or a trampoline floor?

1381. What would be bad about being Prime Minister?

1382. What do you feel is the hardest job in the world and why?

1383. Have you ever been asked to leave a social place like a park or theatre? What happened?

1384. Have you ever lost someone close to you?

1385. Do acts of kindness have a motive?

1386. Who is the first person you text when you get good news?

1387. What's holding you back from pursuing a hobby you'd love to learn?

1388. What are three words that describe your family?

1389. What clothes have you outgrown but found hard to part with?

1390. How can you make a lot of money?

1391. If you had a personal mascot, what would it be?

1392. Do you have a vision of an ideal society? What is it?

1393. It is unethical to eat meat?

1394. How do you handle feeling jealous?

1395. Do you have any scars on your body?

1396. Would you rather mow the lawn with scissors or clean the toilet with a toothbrush?

1397. If money was no object, what would you buy?

1398. Have you ever had a bad accident?

1399. What are your time management skills like?

1400. How many kids did your grandparents have?

1401. What's the biggest surprise you ever received?

1402. Have you ever been on a diet?

1403. If you could drop one activity in your life without consequence, what would it be?

1404. What was the biggest lie you told without getting caught?

1405. Would you have more fun in a pillow fight or a water balloon fight?

1406. What do you think your wedding day will be like?

1407. Which university do you want to go to and why?

1408. Do you have chores at home? What are they?

1409. Would you rather be thirsty or hungry for a day?

1410. What was the funniest thing that happened today?

1411. What do you think would help decrease homelessness?

1412. Do you have enough skill and experience to manage your own home?

1413. Does expecting the unexpected make the unexpected expected?

1414. Are you a good actor?

1415. When you are 80, what will matter the most to you?

1416. What veggie did you hate as a kid?

1417. If you could learn the answer to one question about your future, what would it be?

1418. Do you consider yourself an introvert or an extrovert?

1419. Would you rather be a professor or a reality TV show host?

1420. If someone made a movie about your life, what would you call it?

1421. What did you have as a child that most people didn't?'

1422. What is the most difficult rule to follow in school? Why?

1423. Would you rather give up your favourite food forever or eat cold food for a week?

1424. Who is in your extended family?

1425. Who do you look up to at school? Why do you admire them?

1426. What do you have next to your bed?

1427. What do you enjoy doing for fun?

1428. Can you play a simple tune on the piano?

1429. Would you run away if you could?

1430. What is the most disgusting food combo you've ever seen someone eat?

1431. Have you ever had a paranormal experience?

1432. Would you rather spend all day inside reading or out with friends?

1433. Have you ever dyed your hair?

1434. What makes you dislike people the most?

1435. What's the most meaningful gift you've ever received?

1436. What's the best invention you've seen recently and what do you like about it?

1437. Do you love the city?

1438. What's the most popular TV series among you and your friends?

1439. Are you involved with any community groups or projects?

1440. Who is your favourite superhero?

1441. Which weird animal would you be willing to take on as a pet?

1442. What do you think about eating eggs and dairy?

1443. Do you think that kids and teens should get pocket money? If so, why?

1444. Should people be allowed to live anywhere in the world?

1445. How easy or hard is it for you to touch your toes?

1446. Why do we idolise sports players?

1447. How many 7-year-olds do you think you can handle in a wrestling match before you're overwhelmed by them?

1448. What is everybody talking about right now?

1449. Do you like popping bubble wrap?

1450. What is your favourite thing about your parents' parenting style?

1451. Are adults too serious?

1452. Would you rather meet an evil version of you or a mini version of you?

1453. If you could only eat one type of takeaway food for the rest of your life, which would you choose?

1454. What is your star sign? Do you think your qualities match it?

1455. What do you know about dyslexia?

1456. Do you think there's something that people misunderstand about you?

1457. Do you find it easy or hard to throw out birthday cards?

1458. Do you feel you have too much going on to handle it all well?

1459. Would you skip school with a friend if they instigated it?

1460. What would be different if kids ruled the world?

1461. Who could you be nicer to?

1462. What do you think has been the hardest thing you have ever done?

1463. If your life had a theme song, what would it be and why?

1464. Have you ever had a massage?

1465. Would you rather have a few close friends or many acquaintances?

1466. Which mountain would you most like to climb?

1467. Are you happy with your friendship group or do you want to expand it?

1468. What car will you have as an adult?

1469. What is the first organism to grow back after a fire?

1470. Do we need evidence to know the truth?

1471. Who is a friend you had as a kid that you've lost touch with?

1472. Who was your favourite teacher ever?

1473. What do you think is worth waiting for?

1474. Have you ever had to break up with someone?

1475. What was the last thing you argued with someone about?

1476. Do you make new year's resolutions?

1477. What actor would star as you in the movie of your life?

1478. What is your thinking style?

1479. What would you do if you won the lottery?

1480. What is your favourite thing to do at school?

1481. Have you ever had detention?

1482. If you could change three things about school, what would they be?

1483. Do you want to be more or less like your parents?

1484. Do you have any debts?

1485. If you could describe your childhood in three words, what would they be?

1486. Would you rather eat pancakes for dinner every night or pizza for breakfast every morning?

1487. Which is best, a dream come true or a goal reached?

1488. What are three things you are grateful for in your life, and why?

1489. What is your favourite subject in school?

1490. Would you be happy going naked at a nudist beach?

1491. What do teachers say about you?

1492. What do you think you should learn less of at school?

1493. Would you live on a commune?

1494. How organised are you?

1495. What's the weirdest thing you find attractive in a person?

1496. What are some of the naughty things you did as a kid?

1497. What's the worst part of your day at school?

1498. What is the worst thing about being a teenager?

1499. If you could rummage through a celeb's closet and take anything, whose would it be?

1500. What was your favourite subject through high school?

1501. What is a subject in school that doesn't belong?

1502. Would you go caving?

1503. What do you see yourself doing in 20 years?

1504. What colour do you think your aura is?

1505. What's one thing every human should experience at least once?

1506. What is the best age to get married?

1507. How do you silence your inner critic?

1508. Are we losing our privacy?

1509. What is the biggest risk you've ever taken?

1510. If you had the resources to start a business, what would it be?

1511. Are you an old soul?

1512. If you could befriend one person in history, who would it be?

1513. What do you think it means to be 'male' or 'female'?

1514. If you could go out on a date with a celebrity, who would it be?

1515. Do you like making things?

1516. What is something that has made you angry lately?

1517. Do you think you're hard on yourself?

1518. Which TV family reminds you of your own?

1519. Why should we respect the dead?

1520. Is masculinity a problem in our culture?

1521. What's your Enneagram type?

1522. If your parents wanted to move house, would you want to go?

1523. What do your parents do for a living?

1524. If you were in a horror movie, would you rather be chased by vampires, aliens or ugly creatures?

1525. What is the first thing you do after school every day?

1526. When do you feel peer pressure?

1527. What are three small victories that you've had in the last few days?

1528. What's the best honour or award you ever received?

1529. What makes a person successful?

1530. What was the neighbourhood where you grew up like?

1531. Is war ever worth it?

1532. What would you do differently if you could?

1533. What is something that everyone looks a bit silly doing?

1534. Do opposites attract?

1535. What's your nickname for your best friend?

1536. If a friend makes fun of you, how do you tell them to stop doing it?

1537. What's the next phone you would like to get?

1538. If you were writing the story of your life so far, what chapters would you divide it into?

1539. Have you ever bullied someone?

1540. Are you nice to your parents?

1541. Where were your parents born?

1542. Has a friend ever rejected you? How did you handle it?

1543. What's your biggest pet peeve?

1544. Do you want to live to be 100?

1545. Do you feel confident about your future?

1546. If you could time travel to any year in the past or future, which would you choose?

1547. If you could choose to talk to any animal, which would it be?

1548. Which fruit do you dislike the most, and why?

1549. How high can you count?

1550. Does your family get together for the holidays, and what do you do?

1551. What sport would you choose to compete in at the Olympics?

1552. How would you describe your relationship with your mum?

1553. What would you like more of in the refrigerator?

1554. If you were running for Prime Minister, what would your campaign slogan be?

1555. Who do you love the most?

1556. When you wake up in the morning, what are you most thankful for?

1557. Do you want to move away from your home state when you are an adult?

1558. What do you do when you are alone at home?

1559. Is being tolerant of others important to world peace?

1560. Who is your favourite author right now?

1561. Would you rather your family had more money or more time together?

1562. What is worth taking the time to understand on a deeper level?

1563. What's your favourite taco filling?

1564. If you could only read one book for a whole year, which would you choose?

1565. Have you ever tried your hand at pottery?

1566. Have you ever had a crush on a friend's sibling?

1567. Which of your friends knows the most about art?

1568. What do you think the fourth dimension is?

1569. What do you think should be changed about the education system?

1570. What's more important: science or art?

1571. What's the strangest thing you're afraid of?

1572. If you could be somebody else, who would you choose?

1573. What time do you wake up in the morning and go to bed at night?

1574. Have you ever used a smudge stick? Do you know what one is?

1575. Do you have a favourite domestic animal?

1576. Do you expect to live to be 100?

1577. Can you name the wives of King Henry VIII?

1578. Do you like school?

1579. Would you rather live in a mansion in the city or a cabin in the woods?

1580. Is being middle-class an advantage?

1581. What is the Law of Attraction and does it exist?

1582. Can you be in the wrong place at the right time?

1583. Is your personality similar to someone else in your family, and, if so, in what ways?

1584. What does your name mean?

1585. If you could be any animal, which one would you be?

1586. What do you wish you could learn at school?

1587. What show are you most likely to binge-watch next?

1588. Would you rather spend a day without your phone or without people?

1589. Do you plan to prioritise a career or family?

1590. How do you cope with disappointment?

1591. Why are jokes funny?

1592. What was your favourite TV show when you were 7?

1593. Do you have a favourite poem?

1594. If you could change anything in the world, what three things would you change and why?

1595. What's your favourite childhood memory with your dad?

1596. Are you impatient?

1597. Are you a strong swimmer?

1598. Can you name five constellations in the night sky?

1599. What makes someone a bad friend?

1600. Would you rather live in an RV or a sailboat for the rest of your life?

1601. How do you feel about holding hands or kissing on a date?

1602. Do you have a secret hide-out?

1603. Are your friends from your neighbourhood?

1604. What would you like to invent?

1605. Would you rather wear uncomfortable clothes that look good or plain but comfortable clothes?

1606. What do you dream about?

1607. Do you have a good sense of direction?

1608. Where would you go on a road trip?

1609. Who or what normally wakes you up?

1610. Are you able to get what you need from others?

1611. Who is a pop singer you really don't like listening to?

1612. If you could pick three animals to put together and create a new animal, which animals would you pick? What would it be called?

1613. How do you express anger?

1614. Will you get any pets when you leave home?

1615. How many hours of sleep do you get on average per night?

1616. Are you a songwriter?

1617. Would you rather have a pet dragon or a pet unicorn?

1618. How long do you spend getting ready before leaving the house?

1619. Do you like yourself?

1620. Would you choose never to age if you had the chance?

1621. Did you learn more about life from your mum or your dad?

1622. What's the best part of your day at school?

1623. Do you think that cigarettes and alcohol should be legal?

1624. What things do you joke about that you wish you didn't?

1625. What makes you happiest?

1626. Do you think there is too much technology in the world? What would you get rid of?

1627. Would you rather be the boss or the employee?

1628. What look are you going for when you get dressed?

1629. What is your bedtime routine?

1630. Who was your favourite author as a kid?

1631. What's your favourite national park?

1632. Would you rather have free food from the restaurant of your choice or free internet forever?

1633. What do your parents not know about, that they should?

1634. What do you look for in a boyfriend/girlfriend?

1635. If you could do something illegal without getting caught, what would it be?

1636. Would you rather have no air conditioning or no heating?

1637. What do you like to do with your friends?

1638. What advice would you give to your younger self?

1639. Would you rather have six toes or six fingers?

1640. What is the best conversation topic for the middle of the night?

1641. What hairstyle would you like to try?

1642. Is there such a thing as free will?

1643. Who do you think knows you best?

1644. Do you lie to your parents? What about?

1645. What is the best comeback to say to a bully (without swearing)?

1646. What is a good life?

1647. Who gets it easy?

1648. Which of your relatives had the biggest impact on you as a person?

1649. Which teacher helps you the most?

1650. What's your most loved item of clothing?

1651. What helped you get through COVID?

1652. Are you a capable person?

1653. Would you rather share a room with your sibling or live in the garage?

1654. Would you ever jump out of a plane?

1655. Do you like camping?

1656. Where did you buy your pencil/laptop case from?

1657. Are you a jaw-clencher?

1658. Would you rather ride the bus to school or walk to school?

1659. Do you believe crystals have healing energies?

1660. When you leave high school what will you gladly leave behind?

1661. What's your favourite family recipe?

1662. Which chores are your preference to do?

1663. What's the best museum you ever visited?

1664. What's the weirdest fact you know?

1665. Are choices always good to have?

1666. What do you think makes life easier?

1667. Have you ever felt 'different' in a group setting because of your race/ethnicity?

1668. Who is your favourite internet celebrity?

1669. What is your ultimate goal in life?

1670. At what age do people become mature adults?

1671. What do you think of anti-vaxxers?

1672. Do you prefer the rainforest or the bush?

1673. Do you like surprises?

1674. What's your favourite beach?

1675. Have you ever told a lie that you regret and it keeps coming back to trouble you?

1676. What was the first significant purchase you made for yourself?

1677. What can you remember from when you were 8?

1678. Are you looking forward to creating your first home?

1679. Are you argumentative?

1680. If you go out at night, which is your favourite place to go?

1681. Are you more interested in fame or fortune?

1682. What do you do with your pocket money, if you get any?

1683. What would you rather do by yourself: go to a movie or go for dinner?

1684. Do you ever wish you could go back in time and be a little kid again?

1685. Do you like to accept or question what you are taught?

1686. How frequently do you think you'll see your parents when you are an adult?

1687. What's the most expensive hobby you have?

1688. If you had the power, what would you do about unemployment?

1689. What do you think about too much?

1690. What rights do animals have?

1691. What's a great piece of relationship advice you've been given?

1692. If you could only watch one movie for a year, which would you choose?

1693. Would you rather meet Hugh Jackman or Chris Hemsworth?

1694. If you could set one rule for your family to follow, what would it be?

1695. Do you have any friends you are worried about right now?

1696. Which would you choose: a beach holiday or a snow getaway?

1697. When you are at the park, do you keep your shoes on or take them off?

1698. If there were no restrictions, what would your wildest dream be?

1699. Are you kinder to people or animals?

1700. How can you help someone today?

1701. What is the last thing you wrote by hand?

1702. Would you rather have free Wi-Fi wherever you go or unlimited battery life?

1703. Do you know the name of the language spoken by the First Nations people where you live?

1704. Do you have a favourite band?

1705. What makes someone a hero?

1706. What's unique about you?

1707. Have you ever participated in a protest?

1708. What's the best thing about being a teenager?

1709. Do you have an entrepreneurial spirit?

1710. How old should a kid be when they pack their own lunchbox?

1711. Would you rather warm the bench for a winning team or be the star player on a losing team?

1712. Do your friends and peers date at school?

1713. Do you like jigsaw puzzles?

1714. What is the most dangerous thing you have ever done?

1715. What is something you would change about yourself if you could?

1716. Are you closer to your mum or dad?

1717. Do you believe in God?

1718. Would you prefer to have braids or a buzz cut?

1719. When you study, do you prefer absolute silence or soft music?

1720. What stresses you out?

1721. Do you upload content to TikTok?

1722. Would you rather attend your dream university or be given $200,000 and not go at all?

1723. What was the most challenging part of your day today?

1724. Do you think it's important to have big dreams or better to be a realist?

1725. Do you pray?

1726. What was the most interesting conversation you have ever had?

1727. How would you feel about being an AFL best and fairest player?

1728. What would you call your future dog (or cat)?

1729. Do you prefer art or music?

1730. Is there somewhere you'd refuse to go because of its human rights record?

1731. What should be the name of your generation?

1732. If you knew that the world was going to end soon, what would you do?

1733. What have you learned about yourself in the last year?

1734. Would you rather have all your clothes two sizes too big or one size too small?

1735. If you could choose one comedian to hang out with for a day, who would it be?

1736. What's the craziest thing on your bucket list?

1737. If you had a secret passage in your room, where would it lead?

1738. Can suffering improve a person?

1739. How do you and your friends talk about mental health?

1740. How would you describe your future in three words?

1741. Would you ever have a long-distance relationship?

1742. If someone in your family or extended family was going to be famous, who would it be and why?

1743. Who would you like to run away with?

1744. Have you ever been to Europe?

1745. What is your favourite Sunday afternoon pastime?

1746. How did the world begin?

1747. What's the most useless talent you have?

1748. Do you have superannuation set up?

1749. Would you rather join a choir or a band?

1750. Who is your favourite teacher this year?

1751. What are your pronouns?

1752. Have you ever been wrong about a person?

1753. Do you think you will always live in your hometown?

1754. Would you prefer to snowboard or skateboard if you could be amazing at either?

1755. What car bumper stickers have you seen that you really like?

1756. Do you like the name your parents gave you?

1757. Have you ever been bullied?

1758. How much homework do you get from all your classes?

1759. What was your favourite toy when you were 3?

1760. Would you rather play the role of attractive hero or devious villain?

1761. What is your most prized possession?

1762. What's your catchphrase?

1763. What's something you're looking forward to in the next few days?

1764. As a society, do we care enough about art?

1765. Would you rather have all your food be spicy or sweet?

1766. Would you rather get ten small gifts or one large gift?

1767. Should people travel less?

1768. Can a person be educated without receiving a formal education?

1769. Have your parents or family ever not liked your significant other?

1770. Would you make a good boss?

1771. What is the difference between happiness and contentment?

1772. Can you sew?

1773. What are you knowledgeable about?

1774. Are there parts of your body that you really like?

1775. What pet name does your mum call you?

1776. Do you remember any nursery rhymes from childhood?

1777. Have you ever been to Asia?

1778. What's your favourite summertime activity?

1779. Where do your grandparents come from?

1780. What would you do with a million dollars?

1781. Have you ever stolen?

1782. What is the most boring class you've ever had to attend?

1783. Are you afraid of the dark?

1784. What is the one thing you would change in your life if you could?

1785. How important is physical appearance?

1786. Can you be happy with no money?

1787. What do you do every morning before school?

1788. What is one thing you know you should be able to do by your age, but still can't?

1789. Do you have any dark secrets?

1790. Are you a night owl?

1791. What do you daydream about?

1792. Are there any celebrities that people say you look like?

1793. What do you think of the older generation's attitude to same-sex relationships?

1794. Do you think heartbreak is real?

1795. Is the internet fun or do you feel the downsides outweigh the good?

1796. Would you rather have 20 hobbies or a single passion?

1797. Would you rather read people's minds or read animals' minds?

1798. Do you like working out?

1799. Do you believe in love at first sight?

1800. What questions do you often ask yourself?

1801. What is your biggest hope, and what will you do to make it happen?

1802. Who was your first kiss?

1803. What's the funniest joke you've ever heard?

1804. If you could choose some students in your year to permanently move to Greenland, who would you pick?

1805. What qualities do all of your good friends have in common?

1806. Are you community-spirited?

1807. What do you think your parents like most about you?

1808. What bad habits do you want to break?

1809. If you could invent a machine, what would it do?

1810. Who could you not live without?

1811. Do you 'like' anyone right now?

1812. Why are some people bad losers?

1813. Are you good at debating?

1814. What period in history would you like to live in?

1815. Are you a rational person?

1816. Do you believe in the supernatural?

1817. What's the biggest compliment you have ever received?

1818. Do you prefer the city or the country?

1819. What's your favourite taste?

1820. Do your parents attend all your school and extracurricular events, and do you want them there or not?

1821. What's the most embarrassing thing in your search history?

1822. What do your parents talk to each other about mostly?

1823. How many hours of television do you watch per week?

1824. Would you rather find $40 on the ground or $150 floating in toilet water?

1825. Do you believe in ghosts?

1826. How would you describe your personality?

1827. What are you most afraid of?

1828. Would you rather be allergic to chocolate or bread?

1829. Would you rather be smart or beautiful?

1830. What is the best and worst thing about school?

1831. What's the kindest thing another person has ever done for you?

1832. Are you close to your family?

1833. What qualities does a good scientist have?

1834. Would you rather live without a microwave or a toaster?

1835. How is time an abstract concept?

1836. What genre of books do you most enjoy reading?

1837. What things in life should always be free?

1838. What's the best party you've ever hosted?

1839. If it was raining meatballs, would you eat them?

1840. What would be your perfect weekend away?

1841. Have you ever grown out of a friendship?

1842. Do you brush your teeth before or after breakfast?

1843. What's the most romantic thing another person has done for you?

1844. What team sport would you like to play professionally (if you could succeed at any)?

1845. When do you feel most like yourself?

1846. Do thoughts have a pattern?

1847. Would you rather adopt a child or have your own?

1848. What should a country go to war over?

1849. Do you have a wild side?

1850. What's the worst date you've been on?

1851. Would you rather wear slippers in the bush or gumboots to the beach?

1852. Who was your first crush?

1853. What's your favourite filter on social media?

1854. What would you like to make a movie about?

1855. What makes your family unique?

1856. Do you have a boyfriend or girlfriend?

1857. Did your parents have a name picked out for you if you'd been a different gender?

1858. If you have siblings, do you feel like you're closer with one of them?

1859. What was your favourite book when you were little?

1860. Do you have a green thumb?

1861. Will you be a CEO one day?

1862. Do you play video games, if so which ones?

1863. How do you know when you should get up in the morning?

1864. What TV channels do you watch the most?

1865. Do you like studying?

1866. What's your favourite subject to research and explore?

1867. Will humans be extinct one day?

1868. Do you have a favourite car? If so, what is it?

1869. Has your bestie got the same type of phone as you?

1870. What isn't a subject in school that you think should be?

1871. What's one thing you never get bored of doing?

1872. Would you steal cash from your parents if it was just lying around?

1873. What is art?

1874. What are the most encouraging things your parents have said to you?

1875. Would you rather make the best movie ever or the best album ever?

1876. Should parents get divorced if they don't love each other anymore?

1877. How will your kids' world be different from yours?

1878. Would you rather be an Olympic sprinter or ultra-marathon runner?

1879. Do you prefer to stay in or go out on the weekend?

1880. Do you have good feet?

1881. What is your favourite ice cream topping?

1882. Can you read a map?

1883. If you became Prime Minister tomorrow, what is the first thing you would do?

1884. What song do you know all the words to?

1885. Is there anyone you are jealous of? Why?

1886. Would you rather have your own family reality TV show or band?

1887. Would you like to learn to pilot a plane?

1888. Would you rather walk a tightrope or go free climbing?

1889. What is one thing you hope to accomplish by the end of the year?

1890. Do you remember your dreams?

1891. Have you ever cheated in a test?

1892. What's your relationship really like with your parents?

1893. How many books did you read this summer?

1894. Would you rather live 100 years in the future or 100 years in the past?

1895. Where would you love to go for a family holiday?

1896. Would you rather have a famous family member or be the famous family member?

1897. What keeps you up at night?

1898. Have you ever been in a physical fight?

1899. Would you like to be an influencer?

1900. If you had the power, what would you do about poverty?

1901. What do you lie to yourself about?

1902. What's a food combination you enjoy that others might find weird?

1903. Which of your friends is the funniest?

1904. Have you ever shared your best friend's secrets with anyone else?

1905. Would you defy your parents to go meet a friend they don't approve of?

1906. What is your favourite quote or affirmation?

1907. Is there a higher power?

1908. Do you like card games?

1909. On Twitter, would you rather be Kanye West or Barack Obama?

1910. If you had friends all over the world, how would you keep in touch?

1911. What's your favourite city?

1912. What's something that annoys you about school?

1913. What's the best dream you've ever had?

1914. Are you woke?

1915. If your family had more money, how would you like to use it?

1916. What's bad about being an adult?

1917. What topic could you talk about for hours?

1918. If you designed clothes, what would they look like?

1919. What is the compliment you most commonly receive?

1920. Would you rather get a manicure or a pedicure?

1921. What would people on social media say about you based on your posts?

1922. Is one person's terrorist another person's freedom fighter?

1923. If you had to fight for one global cause for the rest of your life, what would it be?

1924. What is the most useful app?

1925. Do you think aliens exist?

1926. Do you eat a smoothie or drink a smoothie?

1927. What do you take the most photos of?

1928. Why does art matter?

1929. Do you like watching wildlife docos?

1930. What was the best part of your day today?

1931. What are three words that describe your family home?

1932. How do you handle feelings of anger?

1933. What do you think is the meaning of life?

1934. Would you rather eat dinner in a castle or breakfast in a hot air balloon?

1935. Do you prefer your mum or your dad?

1936. Will you be rich one day?

1937. What do you want to be known for?

1938. Would you rather find $50 on the street or have people compliment you for a week?

1939. What advice would you give to younger kids about school?

1940. What is your first memory?

1941. Do we choose what to forget?

1942. What subject do you know well enough that you could teach it to others?

1943. If you could download a skill into your brain instantly, what would it be?

1944. Are team sports better than individual sports?

1945. What is your favourite item of clothing? What do you love about it?

1946. What TV or movie character do you feel a bond with?

1947. Do you prefer a furry, feathery or scaly pet?

1948. Is Valentine's day an opportunity for romance or a waste of money?

1949. Would you rather be a robot or a cyborg?

1950. What is one amazing trait you have that you never talk about?

1951. What is your favourite thing about yourself?

1952. Will you be able to visit the moon affordably one day?

1953. Do you know the meaning of your family name?

1954. If you could stay one age forever, what age would you choose?

1955. Do you accept compliments easily?

1956. Is murder always wrong?

1957. What would you like people to say about you after you die?

1958. What new rule would you create for your parents?

1959. Do you journal?

1960. Do you think you're more creative or more practical?

1961. If you could drive any car you wanted, what would it be?

1962. Do you know the principles of Buddhism?

1963. What are your plans for the future?

1964. Which class or subject did you enjoy most today?

1965. Do you prefer comics or manga?

1966. What is one thing that your teacher could do to make your classes more fun?

1967. Are you scared of shark attacks?

1968. What year were you born?

1969. What's bad about social media?

1970. Do you sometimes need space from your friends?

1971. Would you rather perform at the football grand final or play in it?

1972. What's your favourite possession?

1973. Which would you rather have: $1 million today or 1 cent doubled every day for 30 years?

1974. What is your goal for the next six months?

1975. Is it easy for you to fall asleep?

1976. How do you greet people?

1977. What's your favourite bird?

1978. What do you talk to your parents about mostly?

1979. Do you have any hidden talents?

1980. What makes the world go round?

1981. Would you rather cover yourself in honey or tomato sauce?

1982. What do you wish you could talk to your parents about?

1983. Do you like kids?

1984. When you were young did you prefer dolls or cuddly toys?

1985. What's something you wish adults understood about teenagers today?

1986. Are you fortunate?

1987. Who would you go to if you were feeling desperate?

1988. What makes you smile?

1989. Would you ever pose nude for an artist?

1990. What company would you choose to be a brand ambassador for?

1991. Are you named after anybody in your family?

1992. Do you have a celebrity crush?

1993. What do you see yourself doing in five years?

1994. Who is the strongest man you know?

1995. What career or job do you want to have?

1996. Do your parents limit your phone time?

1997. Who is your favourite YouTuber?

1998. How much would someone have to pay you to eat a raw onion?

1999. What do you think is your best quality?

2000. Would you rather be Greta Thunberg or Miley Cyrus?

2001. Would you swap places with Meghan Markle?

2002. What's the most interesting documentary you have ever seen?

2003. What is the worst atrocity your country has committed?

2004. What's a belief you hold that others often don't agree with?

2005. Do you share a bedroom or have one to yourself?

2006. What's your favourite dessert?

2007. What excites you in everyday life?

2008. Do you have any bad habits you wish you could break? What are they?

2009. What is something everyone in your family agrees on?

2010. What are you uncertain about?

2011. What's the best theme park you've been to?

2012. Are mermaids real?

2013. Do your parents embarrass you?

2014. What names do your family call you?

2015. Are you physically strong?

2016. What do you like doing after school?

2017. What is your current screensaver?

2018. Have you ever mocked a teacher or classmate behind their back?

2019. Do people your age still care about professional sports?

2020. Are drugs and alcohol a problem at your school?

2021. Do you think your parents have a favourite kid?

2022. Would you rather live at Disney World or Sea World?

2023. What do your clothes say about you?

2024. Do you have any pet peeves?

2025. Do you think people can watch too much TV?

2026. What does your family spend money on?

2027. If you could have one superpower, what would it be and why?

2028. What's one song that you'll always remember the words to?

2029. Do you know what a koala sounds like?

2030. At a pool party, do you chill with your friends or play party games?

2031. Have you ever been bitten by an animal?

2032. Would you ever go on a double date with your parents?

2033. What's the last book you read?

2034. Which of your friends is currently your favourite?

2035. Are you a poster or a lurker on social media?

2036. If you could travel back in time to any historical event, what would it be?

2037. Do you prefer imagination or reality?

2038. Where were you born?

2039. Do you still hug your mum?

2040. What do you think is keeping you from complete happiness?

2041. What is the most annoying habit someone can have?

2042. Do you have one or two good friends or a large group of friends?

2043. Should the voting age be lowered to 16?

2044. Have you ever borrowed money (over $50)?

2045. What do you hope never happens?

2046. What do you think can be done about bullying?

2047. Would you rather drink expired milk or eat rotten eggs?

2048. Where do you like to go shopping?

2049. What feelings do you associate with your childhood?

2050. How does your family decide who does the chores?

2051. What emotion do you feel the most?

2052. Where is the best place you've ever seen the sunrise?

2053. Is there anything you would like to learn how to do?

2054. What book has had a big influence on you?

2055. Do your parents stand up for you?

2056. What do you like daydreaming about?

2057. What one thing would you change about your school if you could?

2058. Do you look after plants well?

2059. Do you prefer jumper weather or T-shirt weather?

2060. What is one thing you love about your appearance?

2061. Do you think that children under 10 need mobiles?

2062. What slang word do you wish would come back?

2063. What's the best advice you have ever received?

2064. What do you see yourself doing in 10 years?

2065. What was your grandmother's favourite hobby?

2066. Do you have any recurring nightmares?

2067. How do you imagine the love of your life proposing to you?

2068. Why is the sky blue?

2069. Are you an Alpha personality?

2070. What is your favourite spot to sit at school?

2071. What do you like most about yourself?

2072. Do you agree with the current legal age for driving?

2073. Would you ever go in a hot air balloon?

2074. How would you rate the quality of your friendships?

2075. What were three of the best holidays you ever went on?

2076. Have you ever made up a nickname for yourself?

2077. Do you enjoy going to school games?

2078. Do you like paying for things with cash?

2079. Do you think you've ever been in love?

2080. Will AI replace people one day?

2081. Under what circumstances should you reveal another's secret?

2082. What do you think about vaping?

2083. If you had the power, what would you do to help the planet?

2084. What colour are your eyes?

2085. Do you care what you eat?

2086. If you had a robot to help you with school, but it could only do one task, what would it do?

2087. Are there cliques at your school?

2088. Do you talk during a movie, and if you don't, do you mind if others do?

2089. What is your biggest fear?

2090. Who would you like to help?

2091. Where do you want to go on your next family holiday?

2092. Do you ever check Facebook?

2093. If you could be a fly on the wall, who would you want to eavesdrop on?

2094. Would you rather win *MasterChef* or *Australian Idol*?

2095. Would you rather be the richest person in the world and hate what you do, or have an average wage and love what you do?

2096. When have you had bad luck?

2097. Can you remember your kindergarten teacher?

2098. Have you applied for any school holiday jobs?

2099. Would you ever consult a medium?

2100. What is an epic waste of time?

2101. What's a word you use a lot?

2102. What would you do on a perfect day in your life?

2103. Are you honest on social media?

2104. Are you more of a dog or cat person?

2105. Would you rather be an aeroplane pilot or a scuba diver?

2106. What was the last thing that you bought with your own money?

2107. If you could relive one year of your life which year would you choose?

2108. Is justice more important than mercy?

2109. Do you think of yourself as religious, spiritual or neither?

2110. What was the last movie you saw at the cinema?

2111. How much time do you spend in your bedroom?

2112. Which would you rather never add to your food again: sugar or salt?

2113. What have been the most important moments of your life so far?

2114. Is it our moral obligation to improve ourselves?

2115. What is something that you think kids understand, but adults do not?

2116. What's the best thing about the weekend?

2117. Were you a quiet or difficult baby?

2118. Would you serve in the military if called upon to do so?

2119. If you had to lose a limb, which would you choose?

2120. Where is your phone right now?

2121. Were you in Guides or Scouts?

2122. Can you think of an important turning point in your life?

2123. What was the hardest part of today?

2124. Would you rather miss the punchline of every joke or the ending of every movie?

2125. Is your favourite hobby relaxing or tiring?

2126. Is it OK to lie?

2127. Where did you spend your childhood?

2128. What is your favourite meme and why?

2129. What kind of a parent do you think you will be?

2130. Are you patriotic?

2131. Are you humble?

2132. Would you rather explore space or the deep sea?

2133. What are your favourite family traditions?

2134. Do you still hug your dad?

2135. What cause would turn you into an activist?

2136. Are you usually early or late?

2137. Would you rather have no one in the school ever talk about you or be the centre of gossip?

2138. What's the definition of an alcoholic (in your mind)?

2139. What's your favourite conspiracy theory?

2140. When was the last time you missed a bus, train or plane?

2141. Of the people you know, who has the most beautiful eyes?

2142. What song lyrics make you happy?

2143. Which of your friends is most likely to spend time in jail?

2144. What do you think is the best way to solve conflict?

2145. Do you have a credit card?

2146. Have you ever pretended to be sick just to get sympathy?

2147. Are your parents wealthy?

2148. Do you think marijuana should be legal for people after a certain age?

2149. Who is the author of *The BFG*?

2150. What do you like most about your best friend?

2151. What is the best thing about travel?

2152. Do you practise mindfulness?

2153. Would you ever be vegan?

2154. What do you think intimacy means?

2155. Would you rather sing karaoke or dance in front of your mates?

2156. How old should a kid be when they start doing chores at home?

2157. Do you mind being teased by people who love you?

2158. What do you most regret?

2159. Do you have any friends with disabilities?

2160. What's your favourite thing about winter?

2161. If you could switch places with any person, real or fictional, for a day, who would it be?

2162. Would you rather never do chores again or never do homework again?

2163. What (specifically) do you usually do in front of the mirror?

2164. Why does personal responsibility matter?

2165. Is there a company or organisation you'd love to work for?

2166. What is love?

2167. Do you get along with your siblings?

2168. What's the worst party you've been to and why?

2169. How do you describe joy?

2170. Is graffiti a hobby?

2171. Have you ever experienced heartbreak?

2172. How many social network accounts do you have?

2173. What do you think about the Prime Minister?

2174. Would you rather lose $100 or lose all your contacts?

2175. Would you rather switch wardrobes with your dad or only wear the clothes your grandmother buys for you?

2176. What experiences have made you emotionally stronger?

2177. If you could change anything about your parents, what would it be?

2178. What's one thing you'd never want to change about your school?

2179. What do you think about cryptocurrency? Should it be regulated?

2180. What's your favourite app?

2181. Which family member do you avoid at Christmas?

2182. Is being fit and exercising important to you?

2183. What defines a generous person?

2184. Is there a connection between the teen mental health crisis and social media?

2185. If you could marry any celebrity, who would it be?

2186. What kind of dog would you be?

2187. What's your favourite walk to go on?

2188. What do you remember about your last days at primary school?

2189. What's your go-to karaoke song?

2190. How many bones do sharks have?

2191. What do you like about your daily routine?

2192. What gives you goosebumps?

2193. Would you rather watch the same movie on repeat for the rest of your life or listen to the same ten songs?

2194. If you could live out a story in real life, which would it be?

2195. Which shows are you watching right now?

2196. What would you say are your all-time favourite movies?

2197. Would you rather live on the beach or in the mountains?

2198. Is there a motivational speech that sticks in your mind?

2199. What age will you be when you buy your first house?

2200. Do you prefer team sports or individual challenges like playing chess?

2201. What day of the week were you born on?

2202. What do you think is the best number of children to have?

2203. What do you think are the benefits of being autistic?

2204. What is the best thing that has ever happened to you?

2205. Why do we have dreams?

2206. Can you name three things you can do with bi-carb soda?

2207. Do you know your 'ascendant' star signs?

2208. What makes you feel better when you're feeling down?

2209. Are you a good problem-solver?

2210. Would you rather always have the newest technology or the best food?

2211. Are you a spender or a saver?

2212. Would you rather work for your parents or teach at your high school?

2213. What is the difference between a dream and a goal?

2214. What do you think you should learn more of at school?

2215. Have you ever had to end a friendship? Why?

2216. Do you think Gen Z is different from other generations?

2217. Where do you go when you want peace and solitude?

2218. What's one conspiracy theory you actually believe?

2219. What is the craziest thing you've ever done?

2220. Why is it hard to be a teenager these days?

2221. What do you do and think when you see a homeless person?

2222. Would you become a boy (or girl) for a day, if you had the choice?

2223. Do you dress up or down for events?

2224. Would you rather travel back in time to meet your ancestors or into the future to meet your descendants?

2225. What makes you feel free?

2226. What should the minimum wage be?

2227. How old would you feel if you didn't know how old you are?

2228. What do you think about tattoos?

2229. Do you care about looking after your body?

2230. What colours look good on you?

2231. Do you think the spread of misinformation online is a problem?

2232. Is it fair that some people inherit wealth and others don't?

2233. What's the longest relationship you've been in?

2234. What is the point of religion?

2235. Is movie night better at home or in the movie theatre?

2236. What could you invent that would help your family?

2237. Would you rather never play video games or never use your favourite app again?

2238. Do you prefer sneakers or dressy shoes?

2239. What have you done against your parents' wishes?

2240. What was your first date like?

2241. What's the best practical joke you've ever played?

2242. Have you ever been on a road trip in a van?

2243. How do you show people you care?

2244. Do you plan in advance or save things for the last minute?

2245. Are your parents happy?

2246. Who studies harder than you?

2247. What instrument do you play, or do you want to learn?

2248. What clothes do you think will be fashionable in your kid's time?

2249. Do you keep your bedroom tidy?

2250. Where did you go on your most recent holiday?

2251. Do you have good instincts?

2252. What movie makes you cry?

2253. What is your favourite season of the year, and why?

2254. If you could invent an ice cream flavour what would it be?

2255. Would you rather swim like a fish or fly like a bird?

2256. What are your favourite simple pleasures?

2257. What's the best thing you've ever built or made?

2258. Would you rather do laundry or cook meals for your family?

2259. Would you rather own a coffee shop or own a health food store?

2260. What is the best thing about being a teenager?

2261. What would you set a world record for?

2262. What is the most useful thing you own?

2263. Which of your friends knows the most about the internet?

2264. Would you prefer to come back in your next life as a whale or a dolphin?

2265. If they made a TV show about your school, what would it be called?

2266. Would you go on a date with someone you disagree with about a lot of things?

2267. What's your favourite sport to play?

2268. What makes you feel awkward?

2269. If you could live anywhere in the world, where would it be?

2270. Are you a sociable person?

2271. What social justice issues are you most passionate about?

2272. Are you good at DIY?

2273. Do you persevere with things you're not naturally gifted at?

2274. What makes someone smart?

2275. Have you ever stayed up all night?

2276. How many days before you finish high school?

2277. Are you quick to forgive and forget?

2278. Is there something you want to know about your parents but are too embarrassed to ask?

2279. Would you rather be the smartest person, richest person or hottest person?

2280. Have you ever flirted with your friend's siblings?

2281. Do you think you are funny?

2282. Do you believe in reincarnation?

2283. How important is family to you?

2284. What subjects in school do you enjoy learning about?

2285. Should you be allowed to travel anywhere in the world?

2286. Do you remember a picture book you loved as a young kid?

2287. Would you rather read minds or have read every book in the world?

2288. What did you miss out on as a child?

2289. Do you wish there were any other extracurricular activities?

2290. What are three things you have in common with your mum?

2291. Do animals feel sad?

2292. If you don't do your chores, how do your parents respond?

2293. Are you happy with your body?

2294. Have you watched a movie or read a book forbidden by your parents?

2295. What will you never give up?

2296. How long have you ever gone without showering?

2297. What do you wish you cared less about?

2298. Do men receive enough support for mental health?

2299. What's your favourite dinner that your mum cooks?

2300. If you could turn into any animal which would you choose?

2301. What's something you're really good at in school?

2302. Where do thoughts come from?

2303. What's your party trick?

2304. What was your first day at high school like?

2305. Do you know what 'suffrage' means?

2306. What colour pen do you prefer writing in?

2307. Why do they nail down the lid on a coffin?

2308. When you are at a party, where are you and what are you doing?

2309. What was the last movie you saw?

2310. Do you know your personality type? If so, what is it?

2311. What's had the greatest impact on your life, good or bad, and why?

2312. Did you find it easy to learn to read?

2313. What's surprising about you?

2314. If you had to be a villain from a movie, who would you pick?

2315. What makes a person a good party host?

2316. How would you change the world if you could?

2317. At what age should someone be able to have gender-affirming surgery?

2318. Is your country good?

2319. Would you rather be a gourmet chef or an opera star?

2320. Do you see yourself getting married someday?

2321. If you could keep any animal, real or imaginary, as a pet, which would you choose?

2322. Who is the most beautiful girl at your school?

2323. What do you hope never changes?

2324. Which of your friends knows the most about science?

2325. Have you ever been on a long-haul flight?

2326. Who is the funniest person you know?

2327. Where do you see yourself living in 15 years' time?

2328. Do you have a favourite exotic animal?

2329. Have you ever practised a martial art like karate or judo?

2330. What made you laugh today?

2331. What is your least favourite part of the day?

2332. Would you lie to your parents?

2333. What's something you have done that most people haven't?

2334. Of all the things you are learning at school, what do you think will be most useful to you as an adult?

2335. Are you happy with your hairstyle?

2336. If it were up to you, how would you change the world?

2337. What is the cruellest thing you have witnessed?

2338. How many email accounts do you have?

2339. Would you rather donate all your books or all your clothes?

2340. What is the most embarrassing thing you have ever worn?

2341. If you don't believe in God, do you still think religion has a purpose?

2342. Who are you most grateful to and why?

2343. If you had to change your name, what would your new one be?

2344. If no one was looking, what would you do?

2345. How do you best like helping others?

2346. How would you survive on your own in the bush?

2347. If you could have an unlimited supply of any food for the rest of your life, what would it be?

2348. What would make the world a better place?

2349. Can dreams predict the future?

2350. Is having a big ego a good or bad thing?

2351. Do you wish you could change anything about your friendship group?

2352. Have you ever made a friend online?

2353. If you could use only one word as an insult for the rest of your life, what would it be?

2354. Do you know how to create a budget?

2355. Would you kill 10 people to save 1?

2356. How many cousins do you have?

2357. Are you interested in celebrity?

2358. What's the most enviable thing about you?

2359. Who is your favourite sporting hero?

2360. What are three songs that remind you of your childhood?

2361. How do you know that something is fact rather than opinion?

2362. Do you feel pressure at school?

2363. What television show are you currently watching?

2364. Would you rather have large hands and tiny feet or the opposite?

2365. What do you do when you can't sleep at night?

2366. Do you want to be more like your mum or your dad as an adult?

2367. What do you think is the hardest thing about having kids?

2368. Where in the world would you most like to live?

2369. Do you prefer to type or handwrite?

2370. Who or what is humanity's greatest enemy?

2371. What is the most romantic thing you've done for another person?

2372. Are you in control of your thoughts?

2373. What is something that excites you lately?

2374. What's the toughest part of your day?

2375. Would you help a person you didn't like or who had betrayed you?

2376. What are universal human rights?

2377. If you could come from another country, which would you choose?

2378. What is one wish you want to get fulfilled right now?

2379. Do you think the world expects too much of young people?

2380. Are you jealous of someone because of who they date?

2381. What would you like to change about yourself?

2382. Are you like your Chinese zodiac sign?

2383. Should people be penalised for having an unhealthy lifestyle?

2384. Have you ever been in hospital?

2385. What is the best gift you have ever given?

2386. What makes love last?

2387. Do you often laugh at other people?

2388. Have you ever run a business? Did you make a profit?

2389. What's your all-time favourite class?

2390. Can you describe your favourite colour without naming it?

2391. What's the fanciest event you've ever attended?

2392. Which memories stand out from your favourite family holidays?

2393. Does everything happen by fate?

2394. What's your favourite board game?

2395. Would you rather take part in a food fight or a water balloon fight?

2396. Do your parents have a good marriage?

2397. What do you do every night after school?

2398. Would you rather be born smart or become smart?

2399. What's your favourite dish to cook?

2400. Have you ever fallen in love with someone at first sight?

2401. Is beauty subjective or objective?

2402. Would you like to learn a musical instrument? If so, what?

2403. Do you wish you were different?

2404. How do you like to spend your lunch times?

2405. At what age will you leave home?

2406. What would you miss most if you didn't have electricity anymore?

2407. Are unicorns real?

2408. If you could meet anyone, dead or alive, who would it be?

2409. What dish would you like to try that you never have before?

2410. What is your favourite outfit to wear out?

2411. Can you snap your fingers?

2412. Would you rather read only e-books or read only physical books?

2413. What do you admire most about your mum?

2414. What's your favourite piece of art?

2415. What's the proudest you've ever been of a friend?

2416. Do you know the rules of AFL?

2417. Have you ever regretted not doing something?

2418. What is the most embarrassing thing that your dad does?

2419. Where would you like to live when you're older?

2420. Would you rather never have ice cream or chocolate ever again?

2421. What is the longest you've ever stayed awake?

2422. What are you looking for in a friendship?

2423. What do you think about social status and popularity?

2424. Would you rather maintain a six-foot distance or wear a mask when you meet your friends?

2425. Can you put petrol in the car?

2426. What would you do this year if you knew you couldn't fail?

2427. How do you show love?

2428. What are three unpleasant or annoying habits you have?

2429. Is democracy good?

2430. What is your favourite colour?

2431. Which class are you learning the most in?

2432. What's your favourite song of all time?

2433. Would you rather live in one place for a very long time or in lots of places for shorter periods?

2434. If you could give your parents one thing in the world, what would it be?

2435. Is life fair?

2436. Are you a people-pleaser?

2437. Would you ever lie or cheat to help a friend?

2438. When you go to a fun place, do you prefer to go with friends or alone?

2439. Are you a hugger?

2440. Are you superstitious?

2441. What kind of pyjamas do you wear to bed?

2442. If you could grow up to be famous, what would you be famous for?

2443. Do you take turns cooking in your house? What do you make when it's your turn?

2444. Would you share your favourite clothes with your best friend?

2445. How would you use your superpowers (if you had any)?

2446. What is the most useless invention ever?

2447. What do you feel are the keys to living a great life?

2448. Are you a good listener?

2449. What would you do if you had a crush on your bestie's girl or boyfriend?

2450. Do you know what time you were born?

2451. What do you think it feels like to be in a minority group?

2452. If you could make one rule that everyone in the world had to follow, what would it be?

2453. Why do we do things we don't like to do?

2454. Are you artistic?

2455. Which of your friends do you think will be the richest?

2456. Is life fair?

2457. What is a superstition that you have?

2458. What achievement are you most proud of and why?

2459. Do you have any long-term goals?

2460. Can you say the alphabet backwards?

2461. Do you enjoy cooking?

2462. Do you do any volunteer work?

2463. What's the easiest thing to tick off your bucket list?

2464. Which of your friends is the best actor?

2465. What is one food you would never want to try?

2466. Should people be allowed to keep wild animals as pets?

2467. What's the worst online purchase you've ever made?

2468. Would you rather only use email to communicate or only use voice calls (no video calls)?

2469. Which LEGO Friends set would you choose to be real-life trapped in?

2470. What was the most popular song the year that you were born?

2471. When might you have to be cruel to be kind?

2472. If your family home got destroyed but you could keep three things, what would they be?

2473. What was the worst part of your day today?

2474. What is the best and worst food that your school canteen serves?

2475. Would you rather live in a tent or a cave?

2476. Who do you most value?

2477. Do you know what reiki is?

2478. Are you polite?

2479. Which country do you think has the best government?

2480. What do you like talking about?

2481. Who is someone you admire?

2482. Would you rather break everything you touch or get shocked every time you touch something?

2483. When is power good?

2484. Who was the last person you hugged?

2485. How private is your bedroom?

2486. What is your favourite toy from your childhood?

2487. What do you feel passionately about?

2488. Who do you feel bad for?

2489. What's the best thing about staying in a hotel?

2490. What makes a person beautiful?

2491. Do you know basic first aid?

2492. What is your first memory of your parents?

2493. How many minutes are in one week?

2494. Would you rather have your friends or family be disappointed in you?

2495. What are three very boring sports to you?

2496. What activities make you lose track of time?

2497. If you could change one thing about school, what would it be?

2498. What do you think happens when people have sex?

2499. Who is the strongest woman you know in person?

2500. Do you think socks and slides are a stylish fashion statement or a look that's best left to Justin Bieber?

HERRON

First Published in 2023 by Herron Book Distributors Pty Ltd
14 Manton St
Morningside
QLD 4170
www.herronbooks.com

Captain Honey

Custom book production by Captain Honey Pty Ltd
12 Station Street
Bangalow
NSW 2479
www.captainhoney.com.au

Cataloguing-in-Publication. A catalogue record for this book is available from the National Library of Australia

ISBN: 978-1-922944-23-8

Printed and bound in China

5 4 3 2 1 23 24 25 26 27